Honor

thy

Daughter

Cover painting: *"Unio Mystica"* by A. Andrew Gonzalez
Book & cover design by Mark Plummer

Printed in the United States of America by McNaughton & Gunn, Saline, MI

Ex Libris

Honor thy Daughter

Marilyn Howell

MAPS

The Multidisciplinary Association for Psychedelic Studies

Acknowledgments

THIS BOOK OWES MUCH to the knowledge and unwavering support of many generous people. Thanks to Ann Matranga, superb writing coach and editor of the early drafts; to Ross Gelbspan, who offered excellent advice and constant encouragement; to Anne Gelbspan for her impeccable judgment; to Steven Kotler, Onnesha Roychoudhuri, and Jenny Williams for their thoughtful suggestions; and to Brad Burge, whose editing skill brought clarity and cohesion to the final version.

I especially wish to thank my dear family: Skip, Letty, Brian, Melissa, Niki, and Julian Nault, as well as Julie, Dan, and Mia Montoya.

I am also grateful to the many friends who helped in more ways than I can describe: Julie Anderson, Kira Thaler Marbit, Courtney Walsh, Lindsay Corliss, Dawn Bittman, Joanna Rotkin, Joyce Gallager, Jane Gilman, Don Leka, Marcia Hutchinson, Julia Kirst, Anne Erde, Ann Butler, Lynn Rosenberg, Lee Cook Childs, Barbara Sass, Karen Johnson, Oliver Williams, Mana Washio, and Martha Farlow.

Finally, I wish to express my unending gratitude to the folks at the Multidisciplinary Association for Psychedelic Studies (MAPS) who believed in this book and helped me through the publishing process.

NOTE TO THE READER:
ALTHOUGH THIS IS A TRUE STORY, UNLESS
OTHERWISE NOTED THE NAMES OF
MEDICAL PROFESSIONALS AND THERAPISTS
HAVE BEEN CHANGED TO
PROTECT THEIR PRIVACY AND
THAT OF THEIR PATIENTS.

Honor thy Daughter

Marilyn Howell

Mara Howell

Prologue
1988

"**Mom, did you ever do drugs** when you were in high school?" Mara asked.

She was 15, a junior at Brookline High, well past the peak of adolescent angst. Her chopped hair and bitten fingernails had grown back, she no longer avoided me in the corridors at school, and she had even decided to sign up for the senior science course I taught on the connection between body and mind.

"I don't think any kids at my high school did drugs back then," I said. "I heard stories of kids getting drunk, but the most I ever drank was a sip of my parents' wine. I didn't like the taste."

Mara fixed her eyes on mine. "What about later?"

This was a question I'd anticipated, wondering when she would ask, and I was glad it came when she was mature enough to hear the truth.

"It's a long story." I paused, suddenly a bit unsure of myself, how much to say, where to start. "Let me give you a little backstory first."

Mara raised an eyebrow, but it was clear that she was listening. I went on.

"When I was your age, my chest was actually concave. Lying in a bathtub

I could hold a half cup of water right in there." I pointed to the base of my sternum. "And my ribs were jacked up like this." I held my hands above my lower ribs to show her how they used to be. "I was born that way, with a structural deformity."

Mara looked away and folded her arms as if to protect herself. She seemed to know that she was going to learn more than she bargained for.

"Back in the mid-70s, when I was getting interested in mind-body connections, I went to a workshop taught by a psychotherapist who did 'character analysis,' Ron Kurtz. By looking at people—their posture, the way they moved, the tension in their muscles—he could make some very canny deductions about their personalities and emotional histories, even how old they were when they had traumatic experiences. I asked him what he thought of the dent in my chest and my flared ribs. He claimed unequivocally that when I was still a fetus in the womb, my mother didn't want me, and as a response my chest folded in on itself. Later on as an infant I sensed my mother's disapproval whenever I started to cry and I puffed up my little ribcage to hold back my sobs."

Mara looked at me for a long moment as though she might be about to cry herself. "Did you believe him?" she asked.

"I didn't know what to think. I never heard anything like this in my training to be a biologist. But he shook me up, and he got me to the next step when he suggested some mind-body methods to open up my chest and heal the hurt. I knew I had to find out more. That's when I started Alexander lessons, took Feldenkrais classes, got Rolfed, and went to all kinds of workshops. It was the first time in my life that I felt like a bad student. My teachers kept telling me I had to relax, to stop trying so hard, but I didn't know how. I was like an Energizer bunny running around looking for the off switch. After two years of trying, the pit in my chest was still there and my ribs hadn't budged. At workshops I heard some stories about experiences of people who had used psychedelics. In particular, I heard that LSD psychotherapy might lead to a breakthrough."

"LSD psychotherapy? Now that's a combination I never heard," Mara said. At first I thought she was being sarcastic, but she didn't move an inch from where she was sitting curled up with her legs tucked under her. She was waiting for more.

"Let me give you some context. In the 50s and 60s a certain group of psychiatrists and psychologists used LSD to help their patients uncover the hidden roots of their problems. I did some research and learned that LSD psychotherapy could be a way to get to the truth when your conscious memory is shut down, and that's usually because of trauma."

"Were you scared?"

"Yes, I was. It wasn't that I thought I'd go crazy or jump out a window. It was more like the fear I got the first time I jumped off a high diving board. I got very reasonable before I jumped. I looked down and checked it out, and there was water in the pool and a lifeguard on duty, and I had seen other people go ahead of me, so I let go and made the leap. Since then I've read much more, and the data is clear. LSD is quite safe in a therapeutic setting."

There was a quiet moment. Mara seemed to be taking in the information. I decided to stay quiet and let her ask a question when she was ready.

"So," she said finally, "how did you find your psychedelic lifeguard, and what was it like to jump?"

"Good questions," I said. She was helping me frame my thoughts, like a good partner on a research project.

"I tracked down a person who was familiar with the procedures for LSD psychotherapy and asked him to act as a therapist in my home. He gave me a therapeutic dose of LSD, and he played music tapes he brought with him. I stretched out on the floor with blankets and pillows and put on a blindfold to keep my attention internal. After that his job was to stay by my side, kept me safe, and do what I asked." I stopped for a minute and took a sip of water. I didn't want to hurry ahead; I wanted to stay aligned with Mara.

"Are you ready for what happened?" I asked.

"Yes, I think so," she said. "Keep going."

"About half an hour after I took the drug, I began to wail. It was a sound that had never come out of my mouth before, a chilling sound like a ghost, a banshee. Later on I learned to call it a primal scream, but at the time it was not something I knew about, not at all. I guided my therapist's hand to apply pressure to my rib cage, and I knew exactly what place, what angle, and what pressure I needed. My conscious mind split into two parts, one half of me an observer and the other a suffering infant. I cried more deeply than I ever had before. The pain went into my heart and my chest, and crying was the only way to release it."

Mara could hear the quaver in my voice. She reached out and touched my hand. "It's okay mom. Keep talking."

"The sound changed from a wail to a long, resonating tone, and for four hours I repeated the sound Aaaaah over and over. My identity dissolved, and there were no boundaries between me and my surroundings. I was the sound. I was love. I was peace. Every emotion I had ever felt seemed insignificant by comparison. That's when I really knew what a mystical experience was. It might sound strange to you, but I understood what it meant to be one with God. It had nothing to do with faith or religion or belief. I had experienced God."

I stopped and looked at Mara. "Is this okay? Does this make any sense to you?"

She touched my hand again for just a second. "What happened next?"

"I was so tired after the therapy session that I slept for 12 hours. It wasn't until the next day that I realized what had happened to my body. During the hours I was vocalizing, my ribs had flattened and the pit in my chest had become only half as deep. It was as though the sound of God had come through me to release the infant's grief."

After a long pause Mara asked, "Was Grandma still alive?"

"Yes."

"Did you tell her what happened?"

"I did. It wasn't easy. I said that my life was a search for truth. I told her that I knew she loved me, but I just had to know what she felt about me before I was born. She broke down and admitted that she was angry when she found out she was pregnant, and that she'd hoped for a miscarriage."

The silence was as if the air had been sucked out of the room. I had no idea what Mara was thinking. The late afternoon light that had been spilling through the window was nearly gone. I got up and turned on a lamp, waiting for Mara to say something. Minutes went by before she spoke.

"Thanks for being honest with me, Mom. Can we not talk about this anymore?"

And we didn't—not for a long, long time.

Chapter One
2004

"IT TOOK LONGER—it was more extensive than expected," Dr. Poleka said. He had begun Mara's surgery at 6:30 PM after a full day's work. It was now 11:00 PM. I was home, less than a mile away, clutching the phone.

Dr. Poleka, chief of colorectal surgery at Boston's Beth Israel Deaconess Medical Center, had agreed to perform the operation because it was an emergency, because Mara was so young, and because he was the most experienced colorectal surgeon the hospital had to offer. His words, spoken in monotone, felt like a bludgeon.

"I removed more than three feet of Mara's colon and reattached the two ends. The tumor was spreading like fingers over the surface of adjacent organs. I had to remove her spleen and the tail of her pancreas. There were a number of suspicious looking lymph nodes. I removed twelve of them, but there were several others out of reach behind the aorta – too dangerous to risk…"

It was hard to breathe. I let him keep talking until he stopped, and then said, "Thank you, doctor." Courtesy was all I had left.

I had promised to call Mara's father right away. My hands shook so hard, it took me three tries to dial David's number. When he answered, I could hardly speak.

"She...isn't...okay." I repeated the doctor's information between gasps.

Before Mara went into the emergency room, David and I hadn't talked for a long, long time. As far as I was concerned, it couldn't have been long enough—until this happened.

Now David's voice was a healing force as it touched my ears, and my breath began to even out. He had a deep protective voice; he was the one who would kiss you goodnight and make the monsters go away. "We'll get through this together," he said. My fears quieted for a moment, then exploded again as I hung up.

I had experienced shock before. When I was 16, I had seen my brother's face split open in a car accident. Nothing, however, could have prepared me for Dr. Poleka's call. My heart hammered, and muscle spasms in my limbs brought me to the ground. I lay on the floor jerking and ticking, wondering if I was dying.

I stayed on the floor after the spasms finally ceased. I tried to focus on my breath, then on a mantra, then on a sound, but all I could envision was an image of my daughter's devastated abdomen—her severed pancreas, the empty space where her spleen had been, the unreachable lymph nodes, and the remaining colon stretching diagonally across her small intestines. I saw this interior landscape again and again, as bleak and desolate as an abandoned cave. But strangely, the images brought me back. They made the unthinkable real and allowed me to be rational when it was time to return to the hospital.

At 4:00 AM a nurse called to say that Mara was awake enough to see her parents. I went to the bathroom to splash water on my face and got ready to greet David. I flashed back to the hours before Mara was born— David rushing around the house cursing "Where the hell are the keys?" as I waddled to his rusty old truck to undergo 30 hours of unmedicated labor before finally agreeing to a Caesarian, so tired that I didn't care if I ever woke up just so long as my baby was okay. Now, 32 years later, we were going to the same hospital, scared all over again.

After some confusion outside the hospital trying to find a security guard to let us in we found our way up to her room. She was still too drugged to know what was happening, so we were directed to a waiting room. At the end of a long white hall, we ran into the Harvard medical student who had been assigned Mara as her first patient. I asked the only question that mattered: "Is there any hope? Is there any reason to put her through treatment?"

"Oh yes," she declared. "She's young, she's strong." It was a thin ray of hope.

With the young student's optimistic reply in mind, I was determined to be the one to tell Mara about her operation. She would not hear what I heard the way I had heard it from Dr. Poleka. I knew precisely how stress and fear could suppress the immune system and slow healing. She didn't need to hear a death sentence as she began her recovery from surgery.

I don't remember the exact order of the conversations that morning, but I spoke to Dr. Poleka, the other members of the surgical team, and the attending physician—all of whom would gather around Mara's bed later in the day. I sought out every hopeful or ameliorating fact that could soften the news. I learned that the remaining length of colon was sufficient for her bowels to work again; that although a splenectomy reduces immune function, vaccines could compensate for the loss; and that two-thirds of her pancreas was left intact, enough to perform digestive and hormonal functions. She could heal and feel normal again.

I told the doctors that I was a mind-body teacher and consultant, that I knew my daughter best, and that I wanted to be the first one to talk to her about her surgery. It was important that she be allowed to feel hope. There was no need to tell her everything at once, no need to tell her about the suspicious-looking lymph nodes in hard-to-reach locations where surgery was not an option.

Doctors rarely allow the parent of a competent adult to control the medical information given to the patient. Perhaps it was because Beth Israel Deaconess had one of the first mind-body programs in the country. Perhaps it was because I seemed knowledgeable and confident. Or perhaps the doctors were relieved to be spared the burden of delivering news that was all but a death sentence. They not only agreed to let me speak to Mara first, but they respected my request to offer hope and avoid mentioning the inaccessible lymph nodes for now.

When Mara awoke, we returned to her room. David and I slipped through a curtain that surrounded her bed, where she lay still, pale and listless, elbows bent, palms up, surrendered. She managed a weak smile when she saw us.

"I'm okay," was all she could manage to say.

I said everything I could that might ease the blow of what had been done to her. "You're going to feel normal again," I reassured her.

By the time the doctors came to see her, she was ready. She sat up and said, "I'm going to be the Lance Armstrong of colon cancer."

That was the daughter I knew, the woman who stood straight and tall, the adventurer who climbed mountains with an 80-pound pack on her strong back, the teacher who calmed anxious students with a steady voice, the funny girl who made friends laugh. I pictured healthy Mara with warm brown eyes, a slightly turned up nose, full rosy lips, and a strong, determined chin. Her face, relaxed and open, was framed by a cascade of wavy chestnut hair that fell to her square shoulders.

Her first question for the doctors was, "Will I be able to teach in the fall?"

Dr. Poleka built on the tone of hope and optimism. "It's too early to say. Treatments can make you tired, but if anyone can handle teaching at the same time, it will be you." He was emphatic that her disease be labeled Stage III-C colon cancer, and not Stage IV which we all knew was terminal. He told her that the surgeon who had trained him, a former head of colorectal surgery, had himself been diagnosed with Stage III-C colon cancer. He performed the surgery on his mentor at his mentor's request. "That was 12 years ago," Dr. Poleka said. "I had lunch with him last week."

During the sleepless nights that followed Mara's surgery, the terror of the present dredged up the past.

I lay awake looking at the photos that covered the bedroom walls. There were shots of Mara from infancy to the present, and I could see them even when I closed my eyes, running like a slide show—32 years over and over again.

Look for the happy stuff, I told myself, but the images that came to me only triggered old fears. I saw Mara at 16 in front of the video movie store where she worked, where one night she was held up at gun point. After a policeman drove her home, she described the robbery as if it was an exciting movie.

"The guy came in wearing a mask, pulled out a gun, and told me to empty the cash register. I did exactly what he said." Before I had a chance to tell her to quit the night shift, she said, "He left, I'm fine, and I'm going back to work tomorrow." She liked her co-workers, the independence of earning money, and the opportunity to use her encyclopedic knowledge of movies. Mara had always known how to calm me down.

She endured a more prolonged and serious danger when she was 19 while on an outdoor leadership program in Kenya. Part of the training was a three-day trek through dense bamboo jungle, without guides. Mara's team of five young people made their way along trails forged by Cape buffalo where the bamboo was so dense that there was nowhere to escape if the buffalo attacked. Their survival strategy—make lots of noise to announce their location and keep animals away—didn't work. Brian, the team leader, was attacked by a buffalo and suffered life-threatening injuries, including an open chest wound, broken ribs, head lacerations, and back injuries that made it impossible for him to go on. Someone had to stay the night with him while others went for help, and Mara, who had the most first aid training, was chosen by the group for that perilous role. She used her last clean pair of socks to stop the bleeding from his chest wound, and she stayed awake for 20 hours, banging a pot with a spoon, hoping that the loud clang would work better than last time to scare away the buffalos, elephants, hyenas, and big cats that roamed the territory.

"Without Mara's unflinching care I would not be alive today," Brian later wrote. "She must have been afraid, but I couldn't tell it. Her grace under fire gave me the confidence to focus on surviving."

When she got home, Mara told me about the terror lying beneath her "grace under fire." During the long dark night, she told me, she had to leave Brian's side again and again to relieve her bladder. She peed in a new spot each time until she had marked a territory encircling their tent. She speculated that "having the piss scared out of me" might have helped them survive. She periodically took Brian's vital signs and recorded them in her notebook. Her notes and the survival story later appeared in the National Outdoor Leadership School's first aid manual as a demonstration of how to behave in an emergency situation.

I was thankfully spared knowledge of those events until after they were over and she was safe; not so when she was scared out of her wits on the verge of adolescence. At a time when most of her peers were in a gawky stage with gangly limbs and awkward poses, Mara had well-developed muscles, precocious curves, and a mane of luxuriant waves that swayed when she walked. She was unselfconsciously attractive and self-assured.

George, the pleasant young man who lived on the third floor of our home, never seemed to notice Mara. For two years he rented my in-law unit, an apartment with a shared entry and no locks. We knew him as a polite stranger who played the clarinet and taught at a school for music in Boston. His practice sessions at night and on weekends filled our house with music. It never occurred to me when we passed George on our shared stairway that he would get drunk one night and climb into bed with my 12-year-old daughter while I slept in the next room.

When Mara opened her eyes, the dull moonlight revealed a naked man lying next to her. His eyes were shut, his breathing loud, and his right hand moved rapidly up and down to a beat. Quickly she rolled out of bed, ran to my bedroom, trying not to let her feet make a sound as they hit the floor, and climbed the ladder to my loft bed. She woke me up with a shaky hand on my foot.

"Honey, what is it?"

"Th—th—there's a man in my bed."

"Do you know who it is?" My mind jumped to the only likely suspect. "Is it George?"

"I—I—I don't know."

I sprang into action, guided Mara down the back stairs, and dashed with her out the door. Barefoot in our pajamas, we ran to the police station—half a mile in less than five minutes. I did what the police suggested: I signed a restraining order, returned home with Mara in a police car, and waited downstairs while two officers escorted George out of our house. I promised Mara he would never come back, and I promised myself that I would never rent to a man again. I didn't, but the terror left its mark.

In spite of every strategy I devised to help her heal from that early trauma—therapy, journal writing, art, exercise, and play—Mara's emotional wound kept coming to the surface. By the time she went to high school a year later she (who had never been heavy) carried an extra 30 pounds on her 5-foot 8-inch frame. Her head jutted forward to hide the beginnings of a double chin, and her upper back rounded as though to diminish her breasts. She chopped her beautiful hair into a brush and dyed what was left of it orange on one side and blond on the other. I kept my opinions to myself and hoped the phase would pass, and in part it did. In her sophomore year her hair grew back and her erect posture gradually returned. Her weight continued to seesaw, a barometer of her emotional life. She didn't date and didn't have a boyfriend until she was 25, and even that didn't last long.

In my darkest moments of self-blame, I wondered if the fear and tension Mara held in her abdomen contributed to the disease that later threatened her life. I had failed to protect her when she was young and vulnerable.

I tried to let misery come and go without piling on guilt. Until Mara got sick, I believed that I had let go of the grudges of the past, that teaching and practicing forgiveness and compassion had emptied my mind of old fears and resentments. Now on bad nights (it was always night when these feelings came back) I lay sleepless, deep in self-blame. On good days, I could find mercy when judging myself, and could stand by Mara in the here and now.

Chapter Two

FIVE HOURS OF SURGERY had torn Mara's body to pieces. Before chemotherapy, which the doctors said was Mara's only option, she needed time to heal. As a result her oncology appointment, when we would learn the details of the diagnosis and treatment plan, was scheduled for five weeks later.

Challenges surrounded us from the moment Mara left the operating room. In the early morning hours when Mara was coming out of sedation, a nurse leaned over and brushed her body. Mara's reflexive response to the unexpected touch set off spasms in her back, which in turn pulled on the abdominal muscles that had just been cut and sewn.

The surge of pain she felt, of course, had a simple medical explanation. Yet beneath the simple medical reality was a painful ghost from the past. As she lay in her hospital bed praying that no one would touch her, Mara remembered a meeting she had attended for volunteer counselors at a rape crisis center while she was a college sophomore. Looking around the room, she noticed that most of the volunteers were, like her, overweight. In a flash, it hit her: Her weight and sexuality were connected, both of them tied to vulnerability. The memory of the man in her bed surfaced. When she woke up the morning after the meeting she could hardly stand. It took massage, chiropractic care, therapy, and a leave from school for her muscles to relax again.

In the hospital, Mara was given muscle relaxants and other pain medications for quick relief. After a nurse's surprise touch triggered spasms a second time, we put signs on the door and on top of Mara's bed: "Please don't touch me without asking." In spite of the signs, the hospital staff was in a hurry, and the following day it happened again. At that point, I asked friends who were begging for ways to help to be Mara's bodyguards when neither David nor I could be there. It takes a village, I thought, and I saw that our village was strong.

Mara was used to living with pain. A month earlier she had been a research volunteer in Honduras gathering data on fish populations and earning her scuba certification. She fractured a rib on the second day of the trip as she was hauled over the side of the boat—and kept right on diving for the next ten days.

And that followed what Mara referred to as "my year of pain," the months prior to surgery when a tumor partially blocked her colon. Doctors told her she had irritable bowel syndrome (IBS). She accepted the diagnosis as a fact of her life and kept on going with her chin up, an attitude she must have learned from me. I wonder now whether the blessing of an uncomplaining, sturdy nature—a source of pride for us both—became a curse. If she had whined, screamed, and besieged her HMO to test further, would it have made a difference? For better and for worse, that was not my daughter's way.

Weeks passed and her surgical wounds healed. Mara began to feel better than she had in many months. She stopped taking pain medication two weeks after the operation. Every day she walked further, breathed easier, and slept better. She talked about getting back to her teaching. She was well loved in her private elementary school among staff, students, and parents. The school community bent over backward to find a substitute for her until she could return.

At my home in Brookline, Massachusetts, a tide of visitors started rolling in from California. First to arrive was Annie, my friend from the 60s who had moved to San Francisco. Mara liked to say that Annie was responsible for her existence because it was Annie who introduced me to David, back in the day of Woodstock, cross-country VW bus trips, itinerant musicians, and new friends everywhere. By the time Mara got cancer, my old friend had become Mara's close friend too, as well as her West coast mom.

Annie was a Cambridge hippie when I met her. She was married to Doug, a Unitarian theological student who dropped out of the ministry to fix Volkswagens in a backyard shop. She was petite and proud, and wore jeans and leotards and never a bra. By contrast, I was a refugee from graduate school with a strong athletic body that I didn't always appreciate: I sometimes flelt like a fullback in drag. We met one morning when I woke up in a bed where I'd landed the night before, in a room with a serious slant and ceiling plaster that barely hung on.

"Wake up, honey bunny," said a voice while my short dark hair was ruffled. When I turned my head toward the voice, we both let out a yelp. Annie had thought I was her ex-boyfriend who was living in the back room while I had thought she was my date's undisclosed wife and got ready to bolt. Once we settled our misperceptions, Annie invited me to join her and the guys for breakfast, and our friendship began.

A year later, in 1968, pregnant Annie and Doug met David on a road trip to Florida. Woodstock had lured David north for the summer, and he thought Cambridge would be a good stop before heading home. Annie, who had just given birth, was in no position to entertain him herself.

"Marilyn, you are going to owe me for this one," she said. "If I weren't married, I'd keep this man to myself. He looks great in jeans, and I can only guess…" She left the rest for me to imagine. I had nothing better to do on that hot August afternoon.

"Sure," I said. "Send him over."

He stood in my doorway with a guitar in one hand and a cigarette in the other. We exchanged hellos, and his voice was like a deep chord I could feel in my body. He had strong, muscular arms accentuated by a tight black t-shirt, wild thick black hair, dark brown eyes, a day's growth of beard on a cleft chin, sensual lips, and a half smile. We spent the entire week together before he got in his silver Porsche and headed back to Florida where he had a job as a social worker. Within a year he left that job, came to Boston, and moved in with me. He made me feel beautiful.

Six years later Annie and I were both single parents. Annie stayed friends with both David and me for a while, but by the time she moved to California in 1990, her former husband was dead and she wasn't speaking to David. Feelings had been hurt, and even after the details were forgotten she and David stayed apart. Then everything changed when Mara got sick. As it turned out, the history we shared was bigger than the aches and pains. In the wake of Mara's diagnosis and operation, we three, now in our sixties, were together again.

When Annie came to visit, Mara was feeling good, and the two of them wanted to go shopping. Shopping isn't my thing, but I was up for whatever felt light and happy. David volunteered to be our driver. He honked when he arrived at my house in his scrappy old van with "Fine Carpentry" written on the side.

"There he was," Annie recounted later when we reviewed the day. "Leaning against the van, a cigarette dangling from his mouth, smoldering with that same old good stuff." She said she took one look at him and she wanted a cigarette, even though she had quit smoking 20 years ago. "It's like you want to be young again, and you almost are when you see him."

Not in my eyes: I saw a beer belly, tired eyes, and a restrained smile that hid evidence of dental neglect. I also saw something of myself, a parent racked with grief.

David had no interest in shopping malls, but he was glad to drive us anywhere we wanted to go. Mara was up for the skimpy summer fashions she wouldn't have chosen before her post-surgical weight loss (what she called "the good symptom"). Annie was a crazed shopper, long past her jeans and leotard days. She got a black cocktail dress to wear to a wedding back in California.

"It's my hot mama, elder-babe costume," she said. "It won't work much longer, so carpe diem." As for me, I reserve shopping for when my old t-shirts and jeans begin to disintegrate. Costco is my fashion provider—the same pants and tops in different colors—conveniently available when I buy groceries in bulk.

"I've transcended style," I told Mara.

"No, Mom," she said with a raised eyebrow. "It's more like you're fashion-oblivious."

After Annie returned to California, Mara's friends of her own age came to visit, giving me time to get some serious work done. I put my biology training to use and began to investigate alternative and complementary medicine, along with chemotherapy protocols. I was on the hunt for whatever would give Mara the best chance to survive. I didn't trust individual doctors to know the full range of possible treatments or to always make the right decisions.

The medical community had already failed Mara once, and grievously. Seven months earlier, soon after her abdominal pain began, she had gone to her primary care doctor at Kaiser Permanente in Oakland. At first she was treated with birth control pills for possible endometriosis. That didn't help. Then a scan showed a critical finding—a thickening of the colon wall at the splenic flexure. Mara was told she should have an endoscopy to examine her colon from the inside. A specialist ordered a sigmoidoscopy, after which the diagnostician told Mara, "You have a beautiful pink colon. I'll see you when you're 50." Mara didn't know that a sigmoidoscopy couldn't reach as far as the thickening that showed up on the scan.

How could this be? Was the decision based on the fact that 32-year-olds rarely get colon cancer? Was there an internal cost-management issue that influenced the choice? A colonoscopy, which was a more costly procedure, would have found Mara's tumor, allowing it to have been removed before it broke through the colon wall. Even a medical student would know that the finding on the scan would be out of reach of the sigmoidoscope. The sigmoidoscopy missed Mara's cancer by an inch, and she was misdiagnosed with IBS.

Mara went through months of tests and had begun experimenting with dietary changes for IBS before I found out about the pain. I heard her moan in her sleep when I visited her in California.

"Don't worry, Mom, it's nothing scary," she said. She told me about the doctors she'd seen and the "endoscopy" that had ruled out a cancer diagnosis. I never thought to question the appropriateness of the tests. It never occurred to me that she hadn't actually had a colonoscopy or that the area of thickening revealed on her scan had not been examined. But I did question the diagnosis: I was aware that IBS was often used as a fall-back diagnosis when no clear cause could be found for abdominal pain.

Because Mara's pain was constant and seemed unaffected by stress or diet, I searched for other explanations. Since she had been on an Earth Watch program in Madagascar the previous summer, I suspected parasites and set up an appointment for her with a tropical disease specialist when she returned home from Honduras. She never made it to the appointment. She began bleeding from her colon, went to the emergency room, and finally got the colonoscopy that revealed her cancer.

It wasn't easy to get Mara to go to the emergency room. She was a grown-up, used to making her own decisions. I heard her crying in bed in the middle of the day, and when I asked what was wrong, she told me about the bleeding.

"Mom, don't worry," she said as she had before. "It's nothing serious. I'm just exhausted and I'm tired of being in pain."

When I suggested the emergency room she resisted. "I went to the emergency room last week with a broken rib. They're going to think I'm a hypochondriac—or a victim of domestic violence," she said, trying to smile.

At that moment I knew something was really wrong. "I don't care what anyone thinks," I said. "We're going to the emergency room." She let me bully her into it, an interaction so foreign to our adult relationship that both of us went silent as we walked the half mile to the hospital. I had given up driving years ago, and it was one of the rare times when I wished I had a car.

Our relationship continued to change after the surgery. When I placed a pile of her clothes, laundered and folded, on the couch where she was reading, she commented on the change.

"Thanks, Mom. I seem to have regressed. I'm letting you do all the washing and cooking, and I don't even feel guilty—well, maybe a little bit guilty since I'm telling you."

"I don't mind," I said. "It's normal for adults to regress when they live in their parent's house again. Besides, you have a damn good excuse."

But there was more to it than that. She regretted not telling me about her many months of pain. She knew I would have followed the tests and procedures precisely and insisted on a colonoscopy. An earlier diagnosis of cancer and earlier surgery could have made the difference. Mara was glad I had made her go to the emergency room.

Over and over I repeated to myself, If only I had known she was in pain sooner. Yet I knew that regret would drag me down. I tried to be grateful that Mara wanted me to be a full participant in treatment decisions right now.

Although we would be partners in her care, Mara defined the boundaries. She developed a distinct point of view about what she wanted to know and what she didn't.

"I discovered something unexpected about myself," she said. "I thought that if I ever got sick I'd want to know everything about my care and make all the decisions, but you know what? Right now I'm going to leave the 'knowing everything' to you. I'll tell you what I do want—I want the good news."

She asked for information that would boost her confidence and increase her resolve to get well. It was a relief to know that I had been doing exactly what she wanted from the moment she woke up from surgery, before she had a chance to tell me. As her researcher, I would gather information to make intelligent decisions, and I would filter out the scary stuff (like survival statistics) in my reports back to her.

Intellectually I was up to the job, but the information I found took an emotional toll. My research on alternative approaches left me overwhelmed and disheartened. Well-meaning friends and acquaintances sent information ranging from clinical trials for vaccines, to herbal remedies, dietary prescriptions, colonics, and clinics in Mexico. None of these remedies came with a shred of statistical data or convincing evidence of success with advanced colon cancer. There was no time to go deeper. We were running against the clock, and each tick meant the spread of fiendish cells that couldn't be contained or destroyed.

What I learned about chemotherapy for colon cancer wasn't encouraging, either. The side effects could be severe and only a third of patients actually responded with remission. I wondered how much chemotherapy diminished the quality and length of life for the two-thirds of patients whose cancer did not respond. It seemed that the best that mainstream medicine could offer was a crap shoot with poor odds. The chances of a cure were remote; the chances of doing more harm were great. But Mara was not a statistic. She was my daughter and she wanted—and needed—optimism.

I began to read about the healing power of hope, starting with *The Anatomy of Hope*, a recently published, much praised work by Jerome Groopman that weaves together medical knowledge, case studies, and personal experience. The author lives in my town and is affiliated with both Harvard Medical School and the medical center where Mara had her surgery.

In his book, Dr. Groopman tells the story of a 52-year-old woman diagnosed with metastatic colon cancer and the teenage daughter who accompanied her mother to each appointment. At the time Dr. Groopman was just beginning his career, so he followed the lead of an older physician who always offered the most optimistic spin when talking with patients. He didn't tell patients that treatment was offered only to extend life or that full recovery was never expected. The evasions seemed reasonable to the young Dr. Groopman. The mother could have some time without worry, while the daughter could be spared a spiral of depression that could interfere with her excellent academic performance and chances for a scholarship to an Ivy League school. Eventually, the cancer reached a point where treatment was no longer working and all that could be done was manage her pain. The elder doctor was not available to deliver this news to the mother and daughter, so the task fell to Dr. Groopman. The young girl's anger about not being told the truth from the outset had an enormous impact on Dr. Groopman, leaving him feeling that he and his mentor had betrayed both the patient and her daughter.

Upon reading the story, I wanted to hurl the book across the room. I reeled from the blunt statement that advanced colon cancer is "rarely, if ever, curable." Evidently, in his long career as an oncologist, the author had never heard of a survivor. This was not what I wanted to learn from a book about hope. While Dr. Groopman wrote about his feelings of guilt, I wanted to challenge his perspective. I wondered if the girl benefited from not knowing her mother's incurable prognosis, if she'd gotten a scholarship, if she had enjoyed her time with her mother while the cancer initially responded to treatment. I wondered if she would still have become angry had her mother been told she couldn't be cured at the outset, while she still felt well. Was anger the girl's way of coping with tragedy, her way of being energized, her way to prevent the paralysis of despair?

Dr. Groopman never saw the mother and daughter again. He believed bitterness and mistrust were the final outcome of his early evasions and changed his strategy as a result, telling his next gravely ill patients the cold hard statistics and terrible prognoses for their diseases. But this bluntness also led to regret, as he noted the hopelessness and poor life quality that followed. In the end, he suggested finding a "middle ground where both truth and hope could reside."

Middle ground? How could there be a middle ground for my daughter who didn't want to hear the scary stuff? Truth and hope seemed to reside in parallel universes with no common ground. Under such extreme circumstances, shouldn't hope trump truth to make life bearable?

Dr. Groopman wrote that hope not based in reality is "false hope." The very term infuriated me. Hope is a spark that can start a fire and summon the energy it takes to imagine a good outcome in a bad moment. Didn't Mara deserve that spark while she was feeling well? Calling a patient's hope false seemed condescending and disrespectful—and it scared me too, because if our hope was false, where could we go?

Before I had a chance to hide the book from Mara, she picked it up and turned to the index. When she discovered that all the pages devoted to colon cancer were in a chapter called "True Hope, False Hope," she closed the book.

Mara turned away from questions of life and death and grieved for her more immediate losses. Her periods had stopped many months earlier when she took birth control pills for possible endometriosis. Even though she only took the pills briefly, her menstrual cycle didn't resume. She knew that chemotherapy could permanently destroy her chance to have a child. In a rare meltdown, she cried for the babies she had imagined all her life, and the mother she might not have a chance to be.

She dried her tears and picked herself up only to arrive at another impasse when she lost her home on the West coast. One of two Berkeley roommates moved in with a boyfriend, and the other, a doctoral student, admitted that she didn't think she could prepare for oral examinations while sharing a home with a cancer patient. It was understandable, and it was devastating. I flew to California, packed up Mara's belongings, put them in storage, and got home in time for her first oncology appointment.

When it came to doing what needed to be done, I never missed a beat. But inside, I was in an ocean of pain with waves that kept rolling in fast, one after another, and smashing me down. I needed a place to scream and wail and stomp with ear-shattering volume out of Mara's earshot. I found one when my dear neighbor Julie offered her basement with walls of stone as a "grieving den" to absorb my roars. When fear and grief threatened to spill out in Mara's presence, I had a place to go and let it rip.

At other times my fear came through in conversations with friends and family. In a telephone call with my brother, I tried using humor and bravado to assure him that Mara's disease could be conquered.

"The diagnosis is Stage III-C, not Stage IV, the really scary label," I said. "She's going to beat the shit out of the grim reaper."

Mara chastened me in a soft voice as she entered the room: "Mom, I could become Stage IV."

Chapter Three

It was late August, almost Indian summer in Boston, when we went to the hospital to meet the oncologist. We left home a little early so we could take our time, walking the path along the Muddy River where geese waddled and hissed. In the silence between us my mind began to roam. I noticed that the shimmering leaves on our side of the river moved by us much faster than the static screen of foliage on the opposite bank. Beauty doesn't last, I thought. Time is perceived through movement, it is how we measure life. Our only choice was to keep moving.

We walked on without talking, mother and grown daughter, matching our strides. Anyone would have known we were related by our appearance and our comfort with each other. We smiled at a baby on her mother's back and watched a squirrel get chased by a dog. When we passed under a stone bridge that connects Brookline and Boston, I hooted *whooooo* and Mara answered *yooooou*, making who-you echoes just like we had when she was a child. No one could see our matching abdominal scars, mine a remnant of Mara's birth, hers a souvenir of a much more recent and serious trauma.

Over the previous week we had prepared for the oncology appointment together. We expected to learn the results of diagnostic tests that would guide our decisions from then on. If the unreachable lymph nodes were cancerous, the abdominal scan would tell us. Mara believed all cancerous tissue had been removed and hoped for reassurance. We would face the facts together and ask questions we had prepared together. Mara began to list her questions: What stage is my diagnosis now? What is the treatment? What are the side effects? What are my odds of remission? I could no longer protect Mara from the answers, and I felt as if an earthquake was about to be released inside me.

It was time to tell her what I'd learned from my research: only one-third of patients with Stage III colon cancer responded to chemotherapy. She became very still. I added that maybe that had changed, and that complementary treatments might make a big difference. Besides, I told her, she was much younger and stronger than most patients.

We talked, as best we could, about what our roles would be in the meeting, trying to get on sturdy footing as a team. We decided that I would collect essential information and Mara would keep her hopes intact. In the end we came up with a simple plan: She would leave the room if I had to ask any questions that could heighten her anxiety.

The clinic wasn't crowded when we arrived, and we didn't have a long wait. A female resident spent an hour with Mara. She asked about her medical history, lifestyle, profession, and interests. Mara described her well-balanced diet of organic foods with plenty of fiber and her regular exercise. She had none of the lifestyle risk factors for colon cancer—smoking, drinking, drugs, Twinkies—but she couldn't control her genes. Mara's paternal grandfather had died at age 46 of undiagnosed abdominal cancer. By the time he had surgery, the disease had become so widespread that he was sewn back up and given pain medication until he died.

The resident asked Mara to list her questions for the senior oncologist. Mara began with the one that hurt most. "Will chemotherapy make me sterile, and can my eggs be harvested before treatment begins?"

There go the dreams, I thought, and my own sorrow came right behind like an undertow. Mara wanted to be a mother. Years earlier she had said she would adopt if she didn't marry. The larger question—the one she couldn't ask—was, "Can I survive to raise a child?"

No falling apart now, I told myself. I prayed that the doctor would hear the call for hope in Mara's words.

She asked if it was true that only a third of colon cancer patients who receive chemotherapy have a remission, and I added a series of questions about diet, nutritional supplements, acupuncture, and other forms of complementary care.

We thought we had asked great questions, so we were stunned by the impression they made on Dr. Burke, the senior oncologist. She took one look at the resident's notes and decided that Mara was waffling about chemotherapy. We were no sooner introduced than she leaned forward in her chair, looked intently at Mara, and asked, "Do you know how serious this disease is?"

I could feel the icy chill of Mara's terror as she nodded. It was as though the temperature in the room had dropped 20 degrees. This was not the tone for which we had hoped and planned.

Dr. Burke appeared to be in her late 30s, with short dark hair, a firm voice, and a business-like manner. She answered our questions in short sentences: The chance for remission is one in three. Chemotherapy might or might not result in sterility. Chemotherapy needs to start in less than two weeks, and there is no time to harvest eggs. No, she certainly doesn't recommend dietary supplements, herbs, or special diets. Just follow established nutritional guidelines. Avoid medicinal herbs, since some can actually reduce the effectiveness of chemotherapy. No acupuncture, since Mara had a compromised immune system and was at risk for infection.

If Mara's anger was ice cold, mine was fiery hot. The doctor didn't seem interested in the questions we raised, though she never once said "I don't know." What made it worse was that I knew that in a building less than a block away, the Dana Farber Cancer Institute—one of the most respected cancer centers in the country—acupuncture was offered along with chemotherapy to postoperative cancer patients.

I took a deep breath and jumped in. "Do you know that acupuncturists use sterile needles?" I asked. "Do you know that acupuncture needles are much less invasive than the needles your lab uses to draw blood? Do you know that over 20 acupuncture needles can fit inside one hypodermic needle?"

Even while I spoke, I knew I was going to regret my challenge.

At first, Dr. Burke didn't answer. Then she looked at me hard with a grim face.

"This sounds like New Age thinking," she said. "You know, 'mind over matter, good attitudes cure bad disease.' Let me advise you about the downside of that point of view. When patients get sicker, they're left with the guilty feeling that it's nobody's fault but their own."

Though I agreed with her analysis, it felt pointless to say so—she had still missed my point. This appointment was not going well, and there wasn't a thing I could do. I had no more control over it than I had over Mara's cancer—and we hadn't even gotten to the heart of the matter, the latest diagnostic tests.

"Can we go on to the results?" I asked, trying to keep my voice from shaking.

The scan and blood tests were not definitive, but they were far from reassuring. Mara's CEA count, an indicator of how wide-spread cancer was in her body, was elevated above normal. There was some fluid collection behind her pancreas that was either malignant or a temporary and harmless result of the surgery. The lymph nodes near her pancreas were not too big, but they weren't necessarily normal either. The diagnosis was still Stage III-C, but it could change after the next scan, which was to be scheduled in two to four weeks.

It was clear that Dr. Burke was set on chemotherapy. She recommended a port-a-cath for Mara, a catheter implanted under the skin just below her collar bone where a needle could be inserted without pain for intravenous chemotherapy sessions. She recommended that within two weeks Mara begin the gold standard treatment—a chemical cocktail of Fluorouracil, Leucovorin, and Oxaliplatin.

We talked about insurance issues. I had just learned that chemotherapy could cost between $25,000 and $100,000 per month. Kaiser made it clear that they didn't cover out-of-network care except in an emergency, so unless the HMO could be persuaded that Mara's situation was urgent, she would have to go back to California where she didn't even have a place to live anymore.

"I'd like to have the first round of treatment here," Mara said. "I want to know what it's going to be like to have chemo. Once I know, I can handle it on my own in California."

I asked the doctor whether she would be willing to write to Kaiser and make a case for Mara to stay on the East coast, at least for her first month of treatment.

She said she would and later sent us a copy of her letter to the HMO. It read, in part:

> [We] will start her chemotherapy September 1st. We cannot delay chemotherapy past this point for this 32-year-old woman without endangering her chances for survival.

> Ms. Howell does not have a place to live in California and will need some time to make living arrangements and to establish contact with a trusted oncologist in California in order to facilitate the transition of her care. We ask that you grant this young woman the time she deserves...

We had come to the end of our prepared questions. Mara looked over at me and I nodded. She got up, shook hands with the doctor, and left the room. It was time for me to speak to the doctor without her present. I remember thinking to myself, Be calm, you can do this, you are prepared. I consciously let my shoulders fall and relaxed my jaw. It had been clenched so tight that my teeth hurt.

"What did you mean when you said the lymph nodes were not too big?" I began.

Dr. Burke brought her eyebrows together and looked at me with a level gaze. "They're just under the cutoff point, a tiny fraction below the diameter we definitively label cancer."

"Do you think they're cancerous?"

"Probably."

"Do you have any case studies of people with Mara's diagnosis who have been cured?"

"No. If she gets a remission it won't last. When the cancer starts growing again, it's unlikely that the protocol will be effective a second time. The new cancer cells multiply from resistant cells that survived the first round of chemotherapy."

"You don't think she's going to live very long, do you?"

"No, but miracles do happen."

My heart was beating too fast, and I felt unsteady as I walked back to the waiting room. My fake smile could never fool Mara. The bad news was written all over my old face, the one marked by years I would have given my daughter if I could.

We walked back home along the Muddy River, but it was a darker river now, and I noticed different things—a broken branch with dried leaves dangling from a giant oak, a fish floating belly up at the water's edge, dappled light blocked by a cloud that seemed to follow us. When we got home, Mara slumped in my big leather chair and began to cry.

"What's the point of taking poison?" she asked. "There's zero chance of a cure. Why don't I just forget about chemo, let the cancer do what cancer does, and get it over with?"

What is the right thing to say when the world as you know it falls apart? I needed to be strong; I was the mom.

"This probably isn't the best time to decide," I managed to say calmly. "See how you feel over the next few days, and I promise to support your decision."

In a voice so quiet I could hardly hear her, Mara asked me to leave her alone for a while. I walked across the street to Julie's basement and raged— at Dr. Burke for frightening Mara, at myself for making the doctor even more defensive than she was to begin with, at Kaiser, at cancer, at life, at the uncaring, chaotic, out-of-control universe.

It didn't take Mara long to digest the information from the oncology appointment. She chose chemotherapy, confident that the "gold standard" protocol was the right way to go. It felt good to have made that decision, but the feeling didn't last long. Kaiser denied the doctor's request to grant Mara "the time she deserves." There would be no chemotherapy in Boston. Kaiser informed us matter-of-factly, without regrets or explanation, that they would provide an oncologist, a port-a-cath, and a first round of chemotherapy at Kaiser Oakland starting September 1st. That date was a week away.

Mara and I had no time and no energy to fight. Fighting was David's department. He had already begun searching for a malpractice lawyer, and he added Kaiser's refusal to cover chemotherapy in Boston to his list of grievances. While he ranted with fury, Mara and I made our flight reservations and searched the horizon for something to feel good about. We learned Kaiser would provide the same protocol recommended by the doctors in Boston; we had wondered whether they would refuse even that bit of hope. At a moment when it felt like there was practically nothing we could control, we decided to view that, at least, as a triumph, a small victory to help us stay on track.

In the few days before we had to leave, I narrowed my tasks to a critical few, and number one was letting my school know I wouldn't be back the first week. I was in my second year of semi-retirement—the enviable position of spending as much time as I wanted for one class of 25 students. It was important to continue my work while I supported Mara, for her sake as well as mine. She was fiercely independent. As an adult she rejected any display of my protective instincts, even a momentary gesture. If I held an arm in front of her because a car was speeding through a red light as we were about to cross the street, she'd respond with a firm admonishment: "Mom, I've managed to cross streets by myself without getting run over for most of my life. I don't need your help." I dared not offer to take a leave of absence now. Not only would she consider it an affront to her independence, but a glaring admission that I expected her health to decline soon.

I didn't feel like telling the whole awful story over the phone, so I showed up in person, unannounced. Several of my fellow teachers were milling around when I got to the central office. Two of them greeted me warmly, and one looked at me with such pity that I was stunned and had to hold back tears.

"You know," I said. She nodded and approached me with a hug. She meant well, but I didn't want compassion right then. I just wanted to talk to administrators and get out of there.

I explained the situation more emotionally than I had intended. I tried not to look too closely at the headmaster and the science chairman when they said they'd do absolutely anything to help me get through the coming year. I heard the sorrow in their reassurances and in my own shaky voice as I thanked them. I'd have to find a better way to cope with colleagues' sympathy at school, but for the time being, I told myself to let it go. There will be plenty of time to figure it out later on.

When we left for the airport, Mara and I were as ready as we could be. I picked up my suitcase, turned the key in the door, and looked at Mara. Our eyes met for a moment.

"Let's go, Mom," she said. Her voice was steady. "It's going to be okay."

Chapter Four

WE FLEW TO OAKLAND on the red eye the day before Mara's first oncology appointment at Kaiser.

Mara wanted happy moments, and she went out looking for them. I could see the pleasure in her face when she took the wheel of her car and drove us to her prospective new home. She was back in charge.

Mara hadn't actually seen her new apartment yet. Her feelings upon seeing it, a renovated basement of a house in a leafy Oakland neighborhood, were mixed. I had found the place through a friend, and checked it out two weeks earlier when I had come to clear out Mara's previous apartment and store her belongings. Buddhist prayer flags and rainbow flags welcomed us as we drove through the neighborhood. We met the affable homeowner, herself a cancer survivor, who lived upstairs. Mara's eyes got wider when we walked around to the apartment entrance, where a eucalyptus grove filled the back yard with its scent. Inside the apartment was a different story. The windows didn't open, trees blocked the light, a neon orange wall looked like it could keep you awake at night, pipes were exposed, and the laundry room had no door.

I breathed a sigh of relief when Mara told the owner she wanted to rent the unit. In the same way we bargained for health, we bargained for beauty. We'd find a way to make it work.

Our next stop was Aurora, the private elementary school where Mara had been teaching fourth and fifth graders for the past two years. In spite of the cool morning air, there were beads of sweat glistening on her upper lip. I sensed her queasiness in my own rumbling stomach. For us, teaching was part of our identity. There was so much here for her to lose.

It was a few days before the start of the school year, and we arrived in the middle of a staff planning meeting. There was a moment of stunned silence and then a spontaneous cheer for Mara. I sat frozen, caught between pride and embarrassment, as my daughter took a mock theatrical bow.

We retreated to her old classroom until the meeting was over, keeping our thoughts to ourselves. I did my best to disguise the fears that raced through my mind: She looks so good, so healthy. Did she fool her colleagues? Is their enthusiasm inspiring, or is it a heavily weighted expectation? If Mara felt any similar distress, she didn't show it. She focused on organizing materials for the teacher who would fill in for her while I took in the surroundings.

My favorite view was the wall devoted to the animals of Madagascar. The classroom owed the display to Mara's expedition to study the island's ecology the summer before she got sick. Like me, Mara incorporated her own science adventures into her teaching. Unlike me, her explorations took place outdoors in exotic places. When a student brought in a box of Madagascar tea, covered with printed images of lions, zebras, and other wildlife native to continental Africa—but unknown in Madagascar—Mara created a project on activism. Every child wrote to Celestial Seasonings to explain the error. They made and mailed prototypes for new tea boxes with biologically accurate cover designs. Each letter was answered promptly with a thank-you note and coupons for more tea—and then came the surprise. The company actually redesigned the box, ditching the giraffes and zebras but making the lion even larger than before.

The children loved being activists, and maybe they learned that there can be joy in a process even when the outcome isn't what you hope it will be.

"We did our best to let them know there aren't any lions in Madagascar," Mara told the children. "But they're still lyin' to their customers."

As I studied the classroom wall, my mind did a quick flip from Mara's excellent teaching to her terrible illness. Would she have the outcome she hoped for? What was ahead for us now? It felt that there would never be another happy thought without fear running right at its heels.

When colleagues poured in to see Mara after their meeting, I went to talk to the principal. Bob was a Berkeley radical who became paraplegic after falling out of a tree at age 30. Now in his 50s, he wheeled around the school in a chair. He knew all about overcoming obstacles.

I explained Mara's prognosis in detail, telling him all about the demanding chemotherapy schedule, and her desire to return to teaching as soon as possible. He promised that the school would act as a family to support Mara's recovery.

We both knew that families, no matter how caring, have their challenges, and Mara's situation was a big one. Would she ever be strong enough to come back? What role could she play in the meantime, if any? Who would talk to her students and how much should they be told? How would the children deal with severe illness and possible death? Just beneath the surface of our conversation, there floated a whole host of unasked and unanswered questions. When it was time to leave, I bent to hug Bob goodbye. We clung to each other a few seconds longer than we otherwise might have, transmitting the feelings we couldn't say out loud.

That night we stayed with my friend Annie on her houseboat across the Bay, a setting Mara loved. As much as we wanted to go slow, the tough part of the week was about to begin. The next day Mara had an appointment at Kaiser to install the port-a-cath. We were told that it would be the latest in infusion technology, a "cosmetic" choice that would barely show under her skin. The procedure required more anesthesia and took a lot more time than we had been told to expect. Three hours later, it was all over, and Mara was pale and shaky. We had to pull over on the way home for her to be sick. Perhaps it comforted her to be with Annie and me on the drive, the mothers who had been friends all her life.

The next morning I turned to practical tasks, the stuff I was good at. I called Michael Lerner, a prominent figure in the field of comprehensive care and founder of Commonweal, a health and environmental research center near San Francisco. It was uplifting to discover that he remembered me and my work and that as a result we had a connection. Speaking with such an influential person, I felt a bit of control, a bit of power—things I no longer took for granted.

Soon after Mara's cancer diagnosis, I read Michael's book, *Choices in Healing: Integrating the Best of Conventional and Complementary Approaches to Cancer.* I was grateful for his perspective.

Never give up hope. You can fight for your life, even in the face of tremendous odds. Give yourself permission to hope, even in the face of all the statistics that physicians may present to you. Statistics are only statistics. They are not you. There is no such thing as false hope.

Michael wrote that healing goes beyond curing. Curing can't take place without physical healing. On the other hand, emotional and spiritual healing can take place even when a cure is impossible. He said he believed that certain complementary practices combined with mainstream oncology might tip the balance toward recovery. I wanted to know what Michael had learned about best integrative healing practices in the ten years since his book was published.

We talked on the phone for nearly an hour. Michael recommended a medical consultant, an acupuncturist, and a therapist, all with special skills for helping patients with catastrophic disease. At the end of our conversation I asked him if he knew of anyone with Stage III colon cancer who was either cured or a long-term survivor. He could think of only one, a middle-aged woman who died five years after diagnosis. The emphasis, he advised, should be on quality of life and not just length. I tightened my grip on the phone and tried to keep breathing slowly. For Mara and me, hope for a cure and quality of life were one and the same. I thanked Michael with a heavy heart.

Mara began a routine she would repeat for many weeks: blood tests on Monday and three hours of chemotherapy infusions on Tuesday and Wednesday. Even though she was weary to the bone at the end of the week, I flew home knowing she was where she chose to be, with friends, doing her best to live well. I'd drop everything to be with her if she needed me, but needing me was the last thing she wanted.

Chapter Five

WHEN IT WAS TIME to return to Boston, I discovered that there were two sides to my emotions: dread to leave Mara and relief to be home.

Before I went back to school, I had to let my colleagues know what to do when they saw me. I remembered the look of pity that had shaken my composure when I came to speak with the headmaster. I didn't want pity, tears, commiseration, averted eyes, reassurances, advice, or any other response to Mara's illness from my colleagues at school. To spare them and me, I e-mailed the whole staff: "I look forward to smiling when I see you. Please don't ask me about my daughter." Please don't make me cry. Please don't take away this refuge. But I looked forward to teaching, to having my attention fully occupied in the moment.

The rest of the time, whether I was researching cancer treatments, doing the mindless tasks of daily life, or talking with friends, Mara, or her dad, I ached with worry and yearned for hope.

I was having trouble talking with David. We had formed an immediate unspoken truce when Mara's illness was diagnosed, putting aside old anger and resentment to devote ourselves to what was best for her. Now that truce was crumbling.

While I was in California, David had a follow-up conversation with Mara's surgeon. Dr. Poleka said that Mara's prognosis was "hopeless." He explained that youth is not an advantage because colon cancer spreads much faster in a young, otherwise healthy body.

"If she were my daughter, I'd just take her home and love her," he said.

David knew Mara was fighting tooth-and-nail to regain independence, but his grief was bigger than his sensitivity to her wishes. He began to call her every day. Unable to disguise his anxiety, the comfort went out of his voice, his halting speech produced awkward silences, and his constant attention magnified her fear. She counted on old routines for a sense of normalcy, like his weekly call about a Red Sox game or a great new movie. She tried to tell him not to call so often, but she must not have said it clearly or he just couldn't listen, and finally she took the only step she could think of, to stop answering nine out of ten of his calls. "I'm pissed at him, but I still feel guilty," she admitted to me. I felt murderous. How dare he blast her with his stress when she was in her first month of chemotherapy and eager to have her life back?

Mara, David, and I were repeating an old pattern. Mara didn't feel comfortable saying no to her dad. She didn't want to tell him anything she thought he didn't want to hear. She complained to me instead. She probably exaggerated her woes a bit to vent her frustration and to demonstrate her loyalty to me. I commiserated, magnified his offense in my own mind, and added it to my own storehouse of resentments. Sometimes I suggested, "Be direct with your father. Why don't you tell him?"

"It won't do any good," she'd say in a bossy voice. "He'll just get mad or make me feel guilty." We were back to Mara's early childhood.

David and I divorced when Mara was five. Our deep and passionate early love was followed closely by a deep and passionate betrayal before our daughter's birth. Love and betrayal formed a knot that we could never disentangle. For 32 years we were wounded co-parents living separate lives within a few miles of each other. Of course, our separation and hurt had an effect on our child, and (sensitive, intelligent child that she was) she learned to work with the situation.

Mara's family portrait, pinned to the wall of her third grade classroom, was a drawing divided down the middle by a bold black line. On the left Mara and I held hands. On the right Mara sat behind her dad on a motorcycle.

David was her inspiration for adventure. He took her horseback riding, sailing, and skiing. She loved riding on the back of his motorcycle and watching her classmates stare as they pulled up to school with a roar. I cringed every time she put on her helmet. I was Mara's confidant, the one with whom she could talk about her feelings, her mainstay and anchor. David was the wind in her sails.

David's anger toward me made it difficult for Mara to feel truly safe. He could brood in silence, or he could explode. Though he never exploded at Mara, she witnessed some of our conflicts over the years and saw his anger build to red-faced rage. David is a tall, muscular man. One outburst left a three-foot crack in a door in my house and left Mara in tears. She learned to be an angel with her dad.

Though David was proud to say that Mara never needed discipline, he maintained control with unspoken messages. A grimace or a stern look was all it took for her to comply with his wishes. In fact, Mara's ability to attune to subtle cues extended beyond her dad's domain. She learned to pay close attention to the social code in every situation, and always took care not to step over the line. Sometimes she tried to impose her perception of social standards on me. If my head turned toward her in a movie, as if I were about to whisper, she'd give me the evil eye and immediately shift her attention back to the screen. I'd seen that look from David often enough.

Her attempts to make me conform to her sense of propriety could be amusing. One time Mara answered the door when a former student, Jeff, a musical prodigy and local celebrity, dropped by to give me a music tape he had made for the class. Star-struck, Mara asked him to wait while she got me. I was in the kitchen drinking a beer, reading a *National Enquirer* I'd picked up in the grocery store line.

"Quick," she commanded with a fierce look of disapproval. "Hide it. Jeff is here."

"Honey," I laughed, "I don't care if Jeff knows I'm drinking a beer."

"Not the beer, the *National Enquirer*," she hissed.

I put the paper under a pile of file folders to spare my daughter embarrassment. Her ferocity was startling.

Mara's adolescent relationship with David was strained and distant. She became critical of his romantic life, something she was too young to question while it was happening. During most of her grade-school years,

David had intense relationships with two women at the same time, women Mara believed were both faithful to him. When she was 12, he added a third girlfriend. Mara learned to be tactful, not to mention one woman in front of another. Even before she began to judge her dad's love life, she must have been deeply affected by the discretion it required.

David settled into a committed relationship by the time Mara was in high school, but the damage was done. "I don't like the way dad treats women," she said. "I'm never going to discuss my personal life with him." Mara and David were at their best when they sat side-by-side, in comfortable silence at movies, or cheering in harmony at Red Sox games.

Mara had no trouble facing me, however, and she didn't hold back. I heard "I hate you" and "fuck you" more than once from my teenage girl. I was the person she could go after safely when her hormones or her life seemed out of control. Most of the time, I breathed through the anger, said we'd talk when she calmed down, and let go of the pain.

Mara later referred to her freshman year in high school as her "fucked-up year." She taped a note inside her school lockerthat made my heart thump when I learned about it: "I love my hair, but I hate me." It was an easy step from raging at herself to raging at me. On a bad day she picked on me for physical flaws associated with aging: "You're getting a major frown line." "Your smile lines make you look like a ventriloquist's dummy." "You're getting cellulite on the back of your right leg." The one and only time I fought back, my angry reply came out of left field, and although I intended it as sarcasm, it felt all wrong the minute the words left my mouth.

"Cellulite?" I snapped. "You should live so long." Mara burst into tears. I cried, too—vast, inexplicable tears.

One of the gifts of teaching is that it gives you perspective on your own child. Knowing what I did about the challenges of adolescence for my students and their parents, it was easy to see that Mara's teenage years caused relatively little wear and tear. By the time she was out of college we had matured into a comfortable adult relationship.

When Mara was 24 she came home for a three-year stint. She lived in my third-floor apartment while she got her Master's degree in teaching, and she stayed on through a tough first year as an elementary school teacher in a town 30 miles away. She had too many students with too many special needs in a setting with virtually no support. She put in 12-hour days and never felt like she was getting anywhere.

That final year in Boston, Mara complained to me about her dad more than she ever had before. He expected her to have Sunday dinners with him. The weekend was the only time she could socialize with friends, and she didn't like feeling obliged to give such a big chunk of time to her father every week. She complained when David went on vacations and asked her to take care of his dog. She had to get up at 5 AM, drive to his house to walk the dog before work, and go back again to feed and walk the dog after an exhausting day. She couldn't bring herself to draw limits with him, but I said to myself, She's a grownup, and it's not my business. I held my tongue.

Mara's early disappointment with teaching and the demands on her time led her to California. She was young and strong and ready for change, and the wind was behind her. She had friends in San Francisco. Many of her old friends had gone there to stay, as well as some of mine, making it sometimes seem as though there were a commuter shuttle from Brookline to the Bay. Mara took in the scenes of my childhood with far more joy than I ever had. I grew up near the sandy Pacific beaches, the hills and mountains, the redwood forests, the gentle winters, the scent of eucalyptus, the fog that poured through the Golden Gate like foam from a pitcher—and I left for the east after college without so much as a look behind me. I had difficult relationships with my parents and I wanted to put distance between them and me. For my daughter the Bay Area was heaven and home. She got a job as a substitute teacher, and the next year she was hired to teach at Aurora. Her life was on track.

When Mara went back to California after she got sick, old problems with her father surfaced in a more pressing way. He was scared, and his fear translated into expectations she couldn't handle. He called too often and he planned to visit and stay too long. "A week is plenty long for anyone to visit," she said. This time she gave me permission to talk to him, and my fear coupled with old resentments combined to let some anger fly.

"Mara doesn't want you calling all the time. It makes her cancer even scarier."

"She shouldn't feel that way."

"What about her feelings? Why can't you respect what she wants?"

"I just want to hold my little girl."

"She's not a little girl. She's a woman and she deserves your respect. She told me she doesn't want you visiting for more than a week."

"She didn't tell me that."

"She's never been able to tell you what she really wants. She's afraid you'll get pissed or lay a guilt trip on her. She didn't want to give up her Sunday evenings for you. She hated walking your dog when she had no time for her own life. I'll bet she was glad to get away from you when she moved."

David hung up on me. I yelled at the disconnected phone, broke down in tears, and regretted my outburst. David ignored my plea and made reservations to spend ten days with Mara.

He planned to stay at Annie's, where Mara was living until her apartment was ready. Annie was well aware of my fury at David and the long history of our dysfunctional family patterns. She had been on the outs with him for nearly ten years herself, and now she resigned herself to ten difficult days.

"This is for Mara," she said. "And if he says one negative word it's going to be trouble. God grant me the serenity to keep my big mouth shut."

What happened was a welcome surprise and made me see David's role in a whole new way. Mara was excited to see her Dad from day one. He lifted her spirits and worked like a dog to get her apartment ready for occupancy. He built a beautiful door that fit perfectly into the frame that separated her living space from the musty laundry room. He took her to visit friends and relatives. He was attentive to her subtlest expressions and supported her wishes without a hint of hesitation. Annie, my spy and informer, said she found it hard to believe Mara had ever had trouble telling her dad what she wanted. She wrote:

I think Mara has been highly loyal to you and kept her relationship with her father more or less to herself, and I think it is better than she has led us to believe. Maybe secrecy was her strategy to manage the complexity of the "family ties and unties." It seems unlikely that she moved seamlessly from a negative attitude to the joy I saw on her face when David walked through my door. That was what took my breath away. I misunderstood who her father was to her. He's her warrior, her hero.

When the visit was over, Mara didn't hide her enthusiasm. "We had a great time. Dad was wonderful."

There was more to the change in David and Mara's relationship than just a newfound ability to enjoy their time together. "Our roles have switched," she said. "When Dad depended on me, I felt trapped. Now I'm the one who needs him."

I had to forgive David—and myself. Mara needed us both, and she needed us to be kind to each other.

Chapter Six

Hello friends, family, all loved ones,

*Thought I'd give an update on how I'm doing. This is the first time I've
contacted some of you about what's going on with me lately, so I'll start by
bringing you up to speed. You really are in my thoughts even if I haven't
reached out in a tangible way. So for those of you who don't know yet, I
was diagnosed with colon cancer this summer (a freak genetic thing, almost
unheard of in someone my age). Pretty serious. I had major surgery in July
and began chemotherapy on September 1st.*

*I go in for treatment every other week and am tolerating it well—minimal
side effects that are annoying rather than debilitating. I look well and feel
well (I'm not bald, not vomiting, etc.). I go for walks every day, and if you
were to see me today I don't think you'd have any idea that such things were
going on. A recent PET scan shows active cancer in my abdomen and a tiny
spot on my liver, and this puts me into "Stage IV," not an enviable place to
be. This is difficult to digest since I FEEL FINE!*

My oncologist is doing everything he can to help me from a Western perspective. (Now that I'm stage IV, I get to have another drug, Avastin, that is quite promising, only approved in the US for people in Stage IV. Other countries have been using it for folks in earlier stages.) I have also sought help from various complementary medicine practitioners (acupuncturist, herbalist, private yoga instructor, energy work, massage), am cultivating a practice of meditation, and am (mostly) following a macrobiotic diet.

Eastern medicine considers "incurable" cancer a chronic condition that needs to be managed, like diabetes. (I'm not saying that I don't think I have a shot at being cured.) I recently spoke to a man who has had Stage IV colon cancer for a few years, did chemo, and did and does follow an herbal regimen and feels fine. His cancer is there, but has not spread and does not seem to be affecting him.

Overall, my spirits are high. I break down now and then. I am human! But I gain perspective quickly. I have lived a beautiful life and when my time comes, it comes, and I'm okay with that. That said, I am NOT giving up the fight here. I believe strongly that I have so much going for me, that I can "beat" this thing.

The experience has been a blessing in many ways, forcing me to slow down and examine my life. It's a bit of a cliché perhaps, for someone in my position, but I am learning to appreciate all the little things and recognize the incredible beauty that is in this world.

Every day I hear stories about people who have beaten the odds, who have defied all expectations, people written off by their doctors—given months, even days to live, who pulled through to be cancer free. There is so much power in us that Western medicine doesn't understand or recognize. The power of prayer, the power of intention—many resources can have healing results.

So my request to you (and I know some of you have been doing this already) is to keep me in your thoughts now and then. If you are someone who prays, or who talks to the universe, or who believes in

sending out energy, or whatever, send a little my way when you can.
You could ultimately take some credit for my recovery!

Thank you again for your love and support. If you are receiving this
email it is because you have been important to me in some way. Some
of you I have known briefly, and some I haven't talked to in some
time, but you touched my life in a positive way. Thank you for that.

Peace and Love,
Mara

Mara was notified that she had progressed to Stage IV colon cancer—the
official notification of terminal disease—after five weeks of chemotherapy.
Life extension, not cure, was now the goal of chemotherapy, and Mara
knew it. We were as prepared for the blow as we could be (we even tried to
reframe it as an advantage because her new protocol added Avastin to the
three drugs she had been taking), but the news was devastating. Although
Mara sent me her scan report and we spoke regularly by phone, it was hard
for me to be 3,000 miles away from her.

In the sea of information that surrounds us, we tune into the words and
images that resonate with our hearts. Everywhere I turned, my battered
heart became a receptor for grief and suffering. Whether I focused on
cancer research, cancer treatments, or the normal activities of everyday life,
I found reminders of my worst fears.

I tried to choose uplifting books and films, but it seemed that every one
contained a reference to a fatal cancer or the death of a child. For example,
I went to the theater to watch *Million Dollar Baby*, a film which an early
review had described as a female version of *Rocky*: a celebration of a young
heroine who beat the odds. It was a shock when the plot unfolded, ending
with a 33-year-old woman with a devastating medical condition pleading
for help to die. I was horrified: This was beating the odds? Mara would
soon be 33 and might ask the same of me.

Teaching was my best respite from obsessive worry, and even there
I couldn't escape. I didn't discuss Mara's illness with my students, yet
thoughts of her were part of every day in the classroom, every lesson plan,
and every assignment. After a workshop for parents, a mother of one of my
students confided that her younger daughter had been diagnosed with a

rare cancer two years earlier.

"You can't imagine what it's like to have a child with a terminal disease," she said.

After a pause I said, "Yes, I can." We looked at each other with a series of expressions that I understood as shocked recognition, followed by horror, followed by love.

I poured my energy into a search for alternative and complementary treatments. My number-one selection criterion was the credibility of the person making the suggestion. One recommendation came from Cathy Kerr, a Harvard Medical School teacher and researcher who lives with a "fatal" cancer. Eight years earlier she had been diagnosed with multiple myeloma, a disease with an average survival time of three years. She believed that her practice of *qi gong*, a Chinese healing art, kept her alive and strong enough to continue her research at Harvard Medical School. She gave me a referral for *qi gong* teachers in the San Francisco Bay area to pass along to Mara.

I reported my leads to Mara by email and by phone. She had a great deal of information to process, and there were many options she could either choose to accept or not. Although the decisions would be hers, her trust in me gave my suggestions power, and I felt an enormous responsibility for what I presented. The stakes couldn't have been higher.

At one point, a friend of mine researching complementary medicine at Harvard Medical School told me that he knew of a Tibetan healer with a reputation for curing terminal cancers who would be visiting the San Francisco Bay Area. Mara didn't miss the opportunity. Dr. Dhonden, who had once served as the Dalai Lama's personal physician, gave Mara various foul-tasting herbs rolled into small brown pills and told her to take them at certain times of the day. While I didn't believe that the herbs were likely to make a difference, I was nevertheless entirely willing to consider the possibility that an unconventional treatment could offer my daughter a chance to live. Time was limited, and choices had to be made.

At least on the surface, Mara didn't miss a beat. She worked on having the healthiest possible life. "That's my job," she said. She intended to go into remission and stay there with the aid of complementary therapies until a cure was found. She acted on every lead I passed on to her, from *qi gong* to the recommendations I had gotten from Michael Lerner. She was diligent and disciplined in her fight for life.

Following Michael's suggestions, Mara did three things. She applied to be seen by a physician consultant at the University of California whose advice would not be limited to standard protocols or cost-effective procedures. She also started weekly therapy with a psychologist specializing in life-threatening illnesses and began regular appointments with Richard Hoffman, a practitioner of acupuncture and Chinese herbal medicine specializing in cancer. Mara was building her team.

She had looked death in the eye before—when she was held up at gun point and when she stayed by the side of the wounded man on that long dark night in the African jungle—and she had learned that she was up to the challenge. Then and now, Mara seemed to know instinctively about courage in the face of fear. It wasn't that she lacked fear, but that she worked with it and kept a composed surface.

Though Mara had a history of physical courage, she also had a history of uncertainty in social situations. She wasn't typically one to speak up at public gatherings or reach out for friendship to people she didn't know. Now her life was on the line, and she began stepping up.

Annie saw this change in Mara at a lecture in San Francisco on integrative cancer care. The two introductory speakers were Michael Lerner and Mel Reinhart, the UC physician she hoped would become her consultant and advocate.

"We knew it wasn't going to be easy to clear his wait list, and she needed his attention right away," Annie told me. After the event, Annie wrote:

> It was an awesome sight to watch Mara. She walked up to the podium after the lecture with tall-woman posture, like a dancer, and her long hair was waving down her back. She introduced herself to Reinhart and spent several minutes in conversation. Your girl showed up, and he was riveted. She showed this guy that she's going to make good use of his help. She's a fierce player in her own survival.

Perhaps the biggest shift in Mara was her openness to prayer and her request that friends pray for her. She had grown up in two secular households with parents who had given up prayer long before she was born. When it came to explaining the great mysteries of the universe like life and death (mysteries religion was uniquely set up to solve) she believed that turning to science was far more fruitful than turning to God. In a sense, it wasn't necessary to think about God or prayer until she found herself looking straight in the face of her own mortality. Now that she was suddenly beyond the reach of Western medicine, she wasn't going to pass up the potential power of prayer.

Those who received Mara's request for prayers spread the word. If healing thoughts could be sent and received, then they were flooding in from prayer groups all over the country. At a Catholic Mass in Boston, a priest read from the pulpit, "Blessed Virgin Mary, please intercede to heal Mara Howell." Mara's name was placed on a prayer list at the Unity Church in Asheville, North Carolina. The Aquarian Minyon in Berkeley said a Hebrew prayer for Mara, Native Americans included her name in a sundance ritual in Sedona, Arizona, Buddhist meditators in Hollywood chanted for her, *"nam-myyoho-rebge-kyo,"* and Buddhists on both coasts asked the blue Medicine Buddha to work a miracle for her.

Despite her efforts to focus on hope and healing action, Mara wasn't always able to remain composed. When she occasionally pulled the veil aside for a moment, I got a rare glimpse of the other side of her feelings.

"I cry a little bit every day," she told me by phone. "I sobbed nonstop through my first therapy appointment."

When she talked about her meltdowns, her voice was level. I understood that she was protecting me and, at the same time, herself. I told Mara that I also got scared and cried sometimes but I, too, kept the fear and grief out of my voice. It was as though a serious outpouring of grief could be the crack that would allow a tidal wave of fear to destroy all the barriers we had constructed against it.

There was one conversation when that crack almost opened. Mara had been listening to The Tibetan Book of Living and Dying on tape during her three-hour chemotherapy sessions, and had taken up a quote from Milarepa, the poet saint of Tibet: "My religion is to live—and die—without regret."

"I'm not afraid to die," she said before changing the subject. Her rapid shift seemed to be her way to avoid a discussion about death and dying. I barely managed to hold back my tears and the stream of dark thoughts that accompanied them. What about pain and suffering? What about the loss of everything you cherish in life? How can I help you accept death when I can't stop the panic and helplessness surging through me?

Chapter Seven

I HAD TO SEE MY GIRL to really know how she was doing. Mara picked me up at the Oakland airport the last Friday in October for a weekend visit. We hugged a few seconds longer and a little bit harder than our usual greeting. We were careful with our emotions.

I took in her physical presence as she drove. After three weeks on the second chemotherapy protocol, her hair was still thick and shiny, but her eyebrows were fading and fallen hairs clung to her sweater. She wore turquoise jeans, a magenta shirt, and periwinkle gloves to keep her fingers warm, chilled as they were by the chemotherapy. It was a dramatic change from the plain, earth-tone shades she had favored before she was sick. She made no attempt to disguise the blue plastic Avastin infusion bottle she wore like a fanny pack. I felt bittersweet pride in my daughter's fighting spirit.

Her apartment, too, had been transformed. Now, it was filled with batiks, masks, and indigenous art from her travels, pillows in vibrant colors, plants cascading down from windows and shelves, an altar holding a deep blue Medicine Buddha, and Tibetan prayer flags strung across a window that looked out on a deck and a eucalyptus grove. In the bathroom she had written words on the mirror in pink crayon: love, hope, peace, joy, health. The only sign of grief I saw was my own reflection.

We had a restful afternoon, and I was introduced to another new element in Mara's life, a cat named Isadora. Izzy had long white fur with camel-colored patches and a huge plume of a tail. She sat on Mara's lap during the day and curled up near her head when Mara slept at night. As I petted her a thought jumped into my mind before I could stop it: Some day Izzy might be mine. I quickly pushed the thought away.

At the end of the day Mara's friend and fellow teacher Lindsay arrived. She had a box full of get well cards and checks to help Mara pay for her complementary therapies—gifts from the school community. The big surprise was a shawl in the blues, greens, and purples that had become Mara's favorite colors. It was knit by hand with beads, charms, and tiny bear fetishes woven in. "Every member of the staff and every fifth grader had a hand in this," Lindsay said. She mimed how experienced knitters stood behind non-knitters and enveloped their arms to make their hands do the right thing. We laughed because she made it funny, not sad, and I was grateful to her.

Watching Lindsay was (literally and figuratively) like looking through rose-colored glasses. She had pink tones in her cheeks, auburn hair, and amber flecks in her hazel eyes. Her soft-spoken, gentle manner reminded me of Mara's, though her voice was higher, almost like a child's. She was a practicing Buddhist, and she and Mara had been going to meditation centers together. They were already close before Mara got sick, and Lindsay didn't disappear when the going got tough. She and Mara got together every Wednesday to prepare a macrobiotic meal. I looked at them and noted how much they looked like sisters. It was a comforting thought.

Mara told me that sometimes Lindsay spent the night. "I told her that I wanted Izzy for physical contact," she explained. "I can't even think about dating right now, and I need that closeness from something or someone. Lindsay offered to sleep over with me any time I need comfort." She then looked at me as if trying to assess my reaction.

"Hey, I'm jealous," I said. "You haven't let me cuddle with you since you were a little girl."

"Now's your chance," she said. "The sofa bed has clean sheets, but you can sleep in my bed with Izzy and me."

Sleeping with Mara that night, I remembered her early childhood when our physical contact had been a calming experience in my life. Now I synchronized my breathing with hers as part of a meditation: I inhaled darkness and disease, and exhaled love and light to every part of her body. I felt close and connected to her. There were moments when I believed that love alone could cure her.

I didn't want to disrupt Mara's routine or deplete her energy; her endurance was already diminished by cancer and chemotherapy. We took walks, practiced *qi gong* along with a video tape, played with Izzy, and talked about ordinary things like the movies we'd seen and what our friends were up to. Mara rested while I wrote thank you notes that she signed to those who had sent her get well gifts. It was too hard for her to write to her students about their handmade treasures. She missed them too much.

On Saturday evening we drove across the Bay to enjoy a quiet evening on Annie's houseboat. By now Mara was spending as much time with Annie as I had during our days in Boston. They got together every week for a meal, a walk, or a special event. Mara stayed over the night before Annie's colonoscopy and kept her company when she went in for the procedure. They had evolved a give-and-take that worked for both of them, and I could see that the difference in their ages didn't matter much anymore. In many ways they were like any two close friends taking care of each other. It reassured me when the three of us were together—it was as close to normal as we were going to get.

My Sunday morning flight home to Boston came too soon.

I went back to my classroom, my students, and the practices I had followed for years—exercise at the gym, chiropractic, acupuncture, yoga, and meditation. I also began to attend a weekly healing circle with three close friends. Julie (of the grieving den), Jane, and Tottie were neighbors who offered me love and support. We met at my house on Thursday morning before we took off for work or other activities. We did yoga or meditated together, and I updated them on Mara. For a few weeks, time seemed to stand still, and every element of my routine was a comfort, a promise of normalcy.

One afternoon in mid-November, I was on a pleasant walk around Jamaica Pond—blue skies, crisp New England fall air, and the stark beauty of leafless trees reflected in still water—when my cell phone buzzed.

"Hi, Mom." Mara's voice was shaky, and I felt a chill before she continued. "The chemo isn't working." Her voice faltered for a second. "Dr. Wolf stopped my infusions. He wants to start me on a new drug. I don't know what to do."

The news wasn't entirely unexpected. It had been six weeks since her infusions had started. Mara had been waiting for the results of a CT scan, and she had already expressed her reservations about another round of chemotherapy if the news was bad.

"Chemo is so hard on the body," she wrote in one of her emails. "What if the gold standard didn't work for me? Surely another drug has even less chance of working, otherwise they would have tried it first. Side effects suck, being on chemo forces me to be tied to Oakland on a particular schedule."

The dreaded news of cancer progression was magnified by uncertainty about the next step. I didn't know what to do either. We needed help. We had made a consultation appointment with Dr. Reinhart for early December, but Mara was advised to start CPT-11 (Irinotecan) sooner than that. I called Dr. Reinhart's office to explain the urgency of the situation and convinced them to reschedule our telephone consultation for the Monday after Thanksgiving. In the meantime, I made plans to fly to Oakland for the holiday weekend.

It was Thanksgiving. Though it was supposed to be a time of plenty, Mara was noticeably thinner. Her abundant chestnut hair had thinned and her eyebrows were nearly invisible. Her apartment was cluttered, the floor was dotted with clumps of cat fur, and the plants needed watering. As I tidied up, Mara talked about her loss of energy. She couldn't keep up with everything she was doing. I suggested that she hire someone to clean her apartment. Mara seemed relieved by the idea. We discussed her healing disciplines to figure out what she could let go. She decided to stop practicing *qi gong*. Unlike Cathy Kerr, the Harvard researcher whose story had inspired her, Mara didn't feel the chi moving. There was no nearby class to attend, and she had no one who could share the practice with her and support her belief in its value.

Mara was having a hard time. She said she couldn't even enjoy the 20 pounds she had lost since her diagnosis. At 5-foot-8 and a size six, she looked like a model and attracted attention when she went for a walk.

"Who cares?" she said. "I swear that I'll never mention my weight if I'm healthy again."

Last month I'll bet she would have said "when," I thought to myself. Uncertainty was taking over.

In one vulnerable moment, Mara looked down at her lap as if she were speaking to her cat. "I worry most about you and Dad if I don't make it."

I told her to focus on getting well, and not to worry about us, but the next words out of my mouth took me by surprise.

"You've given me so much. I promise to make the most of it." Mara stayed still, her expression unreadable. It was a holy silence.

If I lose Mara, I will not lose myself, I vowed. I will live to honor her spirit. The silence hung in the air until Mara suggested we have tea.

Sleeping with Mara was not magical this time. To my horror, she was in pain again. I could sense her discomfort and began to have physical symptoms of my own. My upset stomach that night was probably an empathic response. Mara was still experiencing numbness and sensitivity to cold in her lips, a side effect of her chemo infusions. I developed a tic in my upper lip, something I never had before.

We had Thanksgiving dinner at Annie's house with her multigenerational family: her 90-year-old father, her son, her granddaughter, and her cousins. Mara looked gorgeous, and she had a cheerful smile. Her eyebrows were adeptly restored with pencil. It was important for her to be upbeat and strong in the company of those she didn't know well. Annie had prepped everyone, including her elderly father Ben (who, we were warned, was likely to say almost anything) not to bring up Mara's health unless she did. She didn't.

I could imagine how hard it was for Mara as each of us around the table mentioned something we were grateful for. I held my breath as Ben looked at us one by one.

"I'm grateful for..." He took a melodramatic pause. "My great great-granddaughter."

We laughed with relief, but for me it didn't last. I could sense the flip side of our expressions of gratitude.

Everything changes, nothing lasts, I thought.

I must have clenched my teeth, because I broke off the veneer on a front tooth. The next day Mara drove me to her dentist for an emergency appointment. At the dental office, I was asked to fill out a questionnaire on my medical history. Before I realized what I was doing, I checked off the little box next to cancer. I've never had cancer. Empathy was running strong.

It wasn't until I returned home that I realized how much fear and grief

I had been holding in check. I stepped into my house, shut the door, and screamed.

Chapter Eight

Dear Friends,

One of the wonderful things that has happened is the addition of Dr. Mel Reinhart to my "team." He is my "go-to-guy" and has empowered me to be very proactive with my oncologist... (who doesn't seem to do much of anything, but does thankfully comply when I make requests). Last night Mel did something wonderful. He finally silenced the voice of my oncologist in Boston. It's been echoing in my brain for all these months. On my first visit she said, "With Stage III colon cancer, we're going for a cure; with Stage IV we're just looking to extend life." This was difficult to hear at the time and even heavier when my Stage IV diagnosis was confirmed in October. I told Dr. Reinhart when I related my mixed feelings about chemotherapy and he said, "Throw what she said out the window. I can show you a whole bunch of cases of people with metastatic [Stage IV] colon cancer who went into complete remission. If she were a man, I'd call that oncologist a sonofabitch." Love him!

I began to feel as though we were riding a roller coaster with high peaks, rapid dips, and big scary valleys. Bad news and good news, fear and hope came in quick succession. Before Dr. Reinhart joined her team, Mara was worn down, in pain, and uncertain what to do. She needed a highly qualified medical advisor to foresee problems, find strategies to make life more predictable, and keep her believing in a good future. With such an advisor she had a chance to take control of her own ride.

Mara was right to be wary of Kaiser's standard treatments and cost-effective policies. It wasn't a big leap to suggest that managed care, always trying to save a few dollars, had caused her fateful misdiagnosis. What doctor in his or her right mind would choose a diagnostic test that wasn't even capable of viewing the suspicious finding on Mara's scan? The choice of an inadequate, lower-cost procedure seemed like more than just a bad call on the part of one doctor. It had the mark of a systemic problem. How, then, could Mara put full faith in the Kaiser oncologist? We knew that he was bound by managed care guidelines and that they were beyond his control. He was the HMO's doctor first, and Mara's second.

Mara wanted a quarterback who was in her camp with no competing loyalty to a bottom line. We felt good with Dr. Mel Reinhart from the start. He was warm, smart, and respectful. He listened, asked good questions, and made it clear that he was with us in our search for solutions.

Dr. Reinhart focused on immediate concerns—Mara's pain first of all, closely followed by the big question of whether to begin CPT-11 in December. He told us that Mara's pain might not be a direct result of the disease, and recommended several over-the-counter medications to help repair the damage wreaked by two months of chemotherapy. As for the pros and cons of CPT-11, he said that because it was a single drug, the side effects would probably be milder than the four drugs in the last protocol. Besides, he noted, Mara was free to stop taking it any time. Dr. Reinhart was a strategist, and while he followed a logical path and didn't pull a lot of punches, he focused on the good news embedded in every problem. For example, infusions were one day a week for four weeks followed by a two-week break, giving Mara time to explore options beyond the Bay Area.

We dropped the formality and started calling him Mel after our second consultation when he told us what he thought of the Boston oncologist.

"I'd call that oncologist a son of a bitch," he sneered. It was like an invitation to speak our minds, to feel safe with him. He was our guy, our own quarterback, who inspired trust. Mara decided to begin CPT-11.

Two weeks after taking the over-the-counter medications Mel recommended, her pain vanished and her confidence in him soared.

Mel liked to keep a lot of ideas in the pipeline, and his proactive approach to Mara's care lifted our spirits. Every time we had a consultation with him, our knowledge base expanded and we took action. We had Mara's original pathology report checked, we sent her scans to a specialist to find out if she could be a candidate for an advanced surgical technique, and applied for a clinical trial for a colon cancer vaccine at a center in Los Angeles. Mara also began injecting Iscador, an extract of mistletoe used for colon cancer in Germany where studies had demonstrated its benefits.

"You're amazing," Mel told Mara. He said he admired her eagerness to learn and take action, and that boosted her spirits even more. We became an effective team, all of us determined to leave no stone unturned.

As grateful as I was for the boost in Mara's spirits and the end of her pain, deep down I worried that Mel offered no real evidence that a cure was possible. I never forgot the conversation when he offered to show us "a whole bunch of cases of people with metastatic colon cancer who went into complete remission." But complete remission is not the same as a cure. Finding a cure rested on a series of huge improbabilities: that Mara would have a complete remission; that it would last long enough for a cure to be discovered; that she would respond to the curative treatment; that her body would not be unacceptably damaged from all of the treatments; and that she could return to a high quality of life. Mara didn't want to think about the odds. She just wanted to hear a doctor say that a cure was possible. Her life force, her energy to go on, depended on hope. Neither of us wanted to challenge Mel's careful choice of words: "complete remission." Why would we?

I wanted a cure for my daughter more than I had ever wanted anything before, or will again. I would have walked over hot coals. I would have given my life for her without a second thought. At the same time I feared the outcome of Mara's own fierce desire. She was uncompromising. Cure, not remission, was her goal. I recalled something Michael Lerner wrote in *Choices for Healing*: "The successful fight for life is not necessarily waged best by the person with an excessive attachment to the outcome." I heard him loud and clear. Fixation on a goal can fuel anxiety, distract us from living fully in each moment, and make it harder to achieve the outcome we desire. Fear and desire are never far apart. Desire is a double-edged sword.

I hoped we could broaden our focus to healing—the alignment of body, mind, and spirit in a state of inner peace—a process that could take place even if a cure was out of reach. I remembered my phone conversation with Michael Lerner in September and how devastated I'd felt when he suggested that we focus on quality of life. I didn't repeat his words to Mara, knowing full well it implied that there was no cure and that her remaining life might be short. Mara's hope was fragile and precious. I respected her evolving thoughts, and most often (though not always) I believed she would find the best path in her own good time. Who was I to say when that would be?

Dr. Rachel Naomi Remen, Michael Lerner's partner and co-founder of Commonweal's Cancer Help Program, validated my support for Mara's focus on a cure. In her book *My Grandfather's Blessings*, she wrote:

> *The greatest blessings we offer others may be...the courage to support and accompany them as they determine for themselves the strength that will become their refuge and the foundation of their lives. I think it is especially important to believe in someone at a time when they cannot yet believe in themselves. Then your belief will become their lifeline.*

Remen had become Mara's heroine, and her first book, *Kitchen Table Wisdom*, was Mara's favorite. She loved the stories of improbable cures, beating the odds, and Remen's own account of living with a life-threatening disease. Whatever she may have thought of them, Mara didn't mention the stories that spoke of courage, grace, and wisdom in the face of death. The tension between hope for life and acceptance of death—and the possibility that both could be embraced simultaneously—ran through both Lerner's and Remen's writing. I hoped the broad message of healing would take root.

We weren't in a position to spend months or years weighing our alternatives. Now that Mara's new chemotherapy regimen gave her a three-week break between treatment cycles, I sorted through programs and possibilities, hoping to make good use of the upcoming Christmas holiday.

One option stood out, the healing work of John of God, a spiritual healer in Abadiânia, Brazil. John of God (João de Deus) performed actual surgeries on patients who reported no pain or infections as well as what he called "invisible surgeries" which were said to channel spiritual energy. I heard credible stories of healing, and even one case of a verified cure from two trusted sources. But I also knew that there were bound to be remarkable cures among the more than ten million people who had come to John of God over three decades. With no record of success rates or other treatments patients had undergone, it was impossible to know if the celebrated cures were really due to the healing power of John of God. They might well have been the result of spontaneous remissions, placebo effects, or other factors.

Still, I knew that spiritual healing was possible. I could not discount my own healing during a mystical experience. The transformation of my deformed chest took place while I experienced boundless love and unity with all of existence. Somehow I had tapped into a resonance of mind, body, and spirit where miracles were possible.

But above and beyond the hope for a cure for Mara was something that moved me even more. I wanted a big experience with my daughter the adventurer, a real life journey. Here was a chance to combine travel to Brazil with healing. I told my idea to Mara and let her decide.

David had a different idea of what Mara needed. He wanted to help her move past the grinding daily requirements of cancer treatments and health regimens. During a December visit he offered the earthly things the two of them loved most—music, road trips, sports, and laughter. David at his best is a man who burns with life. I think he believed that he could give his daughter that vitality like a life-force infusion. They drove south on Route One where cliffs drop precipitously to the Pacific Ocean. For Mara and David, music was a way to communicate when words failed. They listened to Judy Henske, Howlin' Wolf, and Los Lobos, an eclectic mix of rock and blues. They visited long lost relatives on the California coast, an upbeat family of athletes and teachers. There was no heavy talk about making the most of each moment, no solemn promises to "pray for you every day."

"I felt normal again," Mara told me.

Mara's therapist also saw value in taking things as they came. "You can look beyond the next two weeks," she said after Mara returned from the road trip. "You can make plans for months from now, and change them later if need be."

Upon hearing that, Mara decided to go to her friend Jo's housewarming in Colorado in the spring. In the best of times Mara had been careful with money, but she even bought herself a laptop.

"I'm investing in my future," she explained.

Jo visited Mara in Oakland in late December. Back in college, they'd had a women's rock band, with Jo as the vocalist and Mara playing bass and composing tongue-in-cheek lyrics.

"She danced like a wild woman," Jo told me. I cherished these glimpses of my daughter in her college years, especially since as a child she was embarrassed by my occasional flamboyance. I wonder if she was pleased to outdo me when she was away from home.

When Jo visited, Mara screened videos for her from Aurora's school activities. They watched a play Mara co-directed, and saw the graduation ceremony for her class of fifth-graders. "When I saw those videos, I got it," Jo said. "She was so in her element, and I was excited for her to get back to teaching."

Jo believed that Mara's students were an essential source of healing, but when Jo encouraged her to visit them at school, Mara held back. She was unsure how her students—now in fifth grade—were handling her absence, what it would be like for them to see her now, and how she could help them with their concern for her.

She hadn't been to Aurora for three months. In September she had explained to the fifth graders why they were to have a long-term substitute. They had been her students in fourth grade, and they were attached to her. She told them that she had cancer and had to take medications to get well. She was matter-of-fact and optimistic, and said she hoped to be back teaching in a few months. She never stopped thinking about them, but her instinct was to stay away. Now, with Jo urging her forward, Mara decided to reconnect.

The minute Jo and Mara arrived in the schoolyard, squealing girls surrounded Mara. They wanted hugs. They were eager to touch her and tell her what they'd been doing. The boys were more cautious with their greetings. There was only one reference to her health, when a little girl said, "Mara, you look so pale and your eyes look tired." Mara smiled and joked about going to Mexico or Hawaii when she got the chance.

After a while she followed a group of children who wanted to show her their painting and writings. Instantly Jo was swamped with whispered questions from teachers and administrators: "When will she be back? How is she? How is the chemo going?" They wanted her back; the school wasn't the same without her.

When they returned to the car, Mara was spent. Jo later wrote to me:

She was really upset by the comment about how she looked. She was elated and happy to connect with everyone, but more so, she felt worried about her students and concerned about how they were holding up. She felt self-conscious about looking tired and pale. She wanted to be healthy, she wanted her students to see her healthy. She said the next time she went back to the school she would be healthy, and she would be ready to teach again.

Chapter Nine

"I'VE BEEN THINKING ABOUT going to see John of God," Mara said. "Hoffman told me an amazing story about him." It was our first conversation after Jo's visit and the first time Mara had expressed more than a mild interest in the Brazilian healer.

Richard Hoffman was her acupuncturist, a well-known Bay Area practitioner specializing in treating cancer patients. He was an expert in his particular niche of alternative care and steeped in both mainstream and alternative medical research. When Mara asked him what he thought about John of God, he told her about a colleague who accompanied a seriously ill patient to João's center. The colleague was surprised when the healer selected him for surgery rather than his patient.

"It was surreal," the man said. He stood as if in a dream while João removed tissue from deep in his throat with little bleeding and no pain. When he got back to California a blood test showed that his long-standing thyroid condition had measurably improved.

"Hoffman didn't say I should go to Brazil," Mara said, "But he sure didn't discourage me, as long as it doesn't interrupt chemo. I'm not sure yet, but

I'm thinking about it."

The tipping point came during a three-way conference call with Mel. Up to then, Mara had hesitated to ask Mel what he thought of such an unconventional choice. For one thing, she knew that as consulting physician, he couldn't outright recommend an option with no scientific basis. His response was skillful.

"John of God is in the spiritual realm, out of my area of expertise. However, I'll say this much. I've known a number of people who've gone to John of God, and none have regretted it." I wondered if he believed spiritual healing was possible or if his tacit approval was meant to boost Mara's spirits.

Either way, Mara made up her mind. "Let's go to Brazil after Christmas. I don't know what I believe about João, but I don't want to miss a chance, and—hey—we might as well have an adventure."

At the thought that my adult daughter wanted to have an adventure with me, my heart lifted. With Mara due to arrive in Boston in a few days, I scrambled to get roundtrip tickets to Brazil and arranged for a substitute teacher to cover for me the week after vacation. Mara would have only three days at home in Boston before we took off.

The day after Christmas, Mara guided me through security lines, baggage checks, money exchanges, and ground transportation in Atlanta. She was a cool and sophisticated international traveler, and I was an old homebody mom tagging along with her grown daughter. I made a single contribution when I threw myself between the closing doors of an airport train to make our connecting flight to Brazil. We were on our way to the Casa, the center where João de Deus was said to perform miracles.

After 14 hours in the air with no meals to speak of (unless you count the crust of a microwaved ham pizza), we arrived in São Paulo. While we waited for the flight to Brasilia, we got into the contraband I'd smuggled past security—almonds, dried nori, and one ripe mango. We bought tuna sandwiches at an airport restaurant and wrapped them in sheets of nori. Our weird and salty sandwiches made the smuggled mango more sweet and delicious. Mara passed the time studying the Portuguese-English dictionary. She entertained me with English terms that get really complicated in Portuguese translation, like banana split: *banana cortada ao comprido com gelado e nozes e coberta de calda de fruta ou de chocolate.*

I'm not crazy about flying, especially not in tiny airplanes that get tossed in the wind, but I had no qualms about stepping aboard the 24-passenger, propeller-driven plane to Brasilia. Current reality put all other concerns into perspective, and I felt only relief to be on the last leg of our flight. We were well on our way to Abadiânia, a town in the remote high planes of central Brazil. Luck was with us. The flight had no stomach-heaving bumps, our baggage arrived without mishap, and cabs were waiting. The only remaining challenge was to identify our driver. Mara approached a small dark man who held a sign that said "Merlin." Sure enough, he was our cab driver, and Merlin was me, Marilyn. Merlin the magician—yes, I thought, and hoped it was a magical sign.

The two-hour drive gave us a close look at the patches of red and green we had viewed from the air. Red earth and tile roofs alternated with dense foliage and grassy fields. We saw stucco houses in disrepair and ramshackle buildings pieced together from scrap metal, boards, and sheets of plastic. There were long stretches of farmland, lime green pastures with grazing livestock, and bright roadside wildflowers.

The road through Abadiânia was a line of demarcation between two worlds that never met. The west side was the tough part of town. Policing was negligible, we were told, and tourists ventured there at their peril. On the other side was the Casa. The story went that it was enveloped by an "energy bubble" that protected all who entered. Everything on the Casa side of Abadiânia, including *pousadas* (hotels), homes, and businesses were connected to the Casa. We, of course, were advised to stay on the sacred side of the road.

I was struck by the parallel between the split town and my divided self. My mystical side was a place of hope where magic and miracles were possible. My rational side was a dangerous territory fraught with fear, dominated by thoughts of poisonous interventions and overwhelming odds against my daughter's survival.

I cringed at the idea of an energy bubble or anything else that smelled like wishful thinking. At the same time, I had another, opposite concern: My rational mind, trained to spot delusions, might be an impediment to spiritual healing. How could I turn off my bullshit detector and stay open to a realm of experience that goes beyond science? I would do my best to rein in my skepticism and have hope.

We stayed at the Amazonia, a bright coral-colored *pousada* where we had a small room off a courtyard filled with exotic plants. A gangly boy with braces and a fuzzy upper lip greeted us. His English was good, spoken in the cracking voice of an adolescent. He led us to our room to drop off our baggage and invited us to enjoy our first meal.

It was a "fabulous buffet dinner that knocked our socks off," Mara observed, adding that after 24 hours in transit, our socks were "not so fabulous." I recorded this and more in our journal. Since Mara didn't feel like writing, I became her scribe. The journal became our joint record, with my reflections on the left-hand pages, and her dictations on the right.

After dinner we headed for the Casa, a two-minute walk from our *pousada*. It was a large compound, several buildings and gardens surrounded by a stucco wall. We wandered through a large assembly hall that was open to a courtyard on one side and filled with rows of chairs facing a stage. The walls were decorated with pictures of saints, the Dalai Lama, photos of João with honorary guests, and letters of gratitude. A letter from Alberto Fujimori, the president of Peru, thanked João for saving his son's life. We passed a room filled with wheelchairs and crutches left as mementos by those who had been healed. My mind flipped back and forth as I viewed the displays: were they evidence of miracles or persuasive props?

At seven o'clock we gathered with about 40 other newcomers for an English language orientation. We sat at picnic tables in a plaza next to the building where soup was made fresh every day and given to us as true guests at no cost.

Over 200 workers and volunteers like Arturo, our orientation guide, were known as Children of the House. They provided services at the Casa either because they had been healed themselves or because someone they loved had been healed. We were all free to give a donation, and many did, but none of us paid a fee or felt pressure to do so. The Casa functions on the premise that João's care and healing are given freely to all who ask. The Children of the House came from many occupations, races, and religions.

Arturo explained that João was a medium who communicated with spirits and served as a vessel through which God healed. João "incorporates" the spirits of more than 30 individuals, and these entities embody João one at a time when their particular expertise is needed; in other words, the entities take control of João's mind and body. (The term "possession" isn't used, though it might seem to apply here.) The entities are described as doctors, scientists, lawyers, and theologians who led remarkable lives such as Dom Inacio de Loyola, who founded the Jesuit order of the Roman

Catholic Church in the 1500s.

Most of the operations the entities perform through João are invisible, meaning that an observer doesn't see anything take place. There are also a smaller number of visible surgeries performed with surgical instruments without anesthesia or antiseptic precautions. Arturo told us that invisible surgeries are as powerful as visible ones. He said that João performs visible surgeries because, for many people, seeing is believing.

I listened to the information Arturo provided from multiple perspectives— as the skeptical debunker, as the scientific thinker aware of the potential power of placebos, as the pilgrim seeking spiritual healing, and as a mother. The mother and the scientist were locked in combat. It was as though I had my own supply of entities, and they were not easily unified.

Debunking was easy. From a Western medical perspective, John of God had a dissociative disorder. The entities were alternative selves that psychiatrists used to refer to as multiple personalities. I speculated that João went into trance and unconsciously induced hypnotic anesthesia in his patients. A study at the São Paulo University School of Medicine concluded that the incisions he made were real, painless, and caused no apparent infections. However, the tissues he removed showed no sign of disease, and there was no follow-up study to learn whether patients improved. I concluded that João was sincere and caused no harm. I also believed that his "placebo surgeries"—whether visible or invisible—might trigger actual healing.

Suggestion and expectation are powerful forces, the magic that science recognizes but cannot explain. No one knows how beliefs sometimes change the course of a disease, only that they can. Faith in placebo healing—belief in the power of belief—was the compromise I made to resolve my inner conflict. I didn't tell Mara; I wanted to allow her the possibility of accepting João as a spiritual healer, and she seemed to want that, too.

When we returned to our *pousada* after orientation, Mara said, "I still don't know what to believe but I want to be open."

I told her about the psychologist William James, who as a young man suffered from physical illness and depression and was obsessed with uncertainty about the notion of free will. A turning point came when he realized that he could choose what to believe: "My first act of free will shall be to believe in free will."

Mara and I agreed to cultivate belief in João while we stayed at the Casa.

We would observe guidelines, follow rituals, and suspend doubt.

Wednesday morning we put on white clothing, the only dress requirement for all of us at the Casa. We joined hundreds of others wearing pants, skirts, shirts and dresses in every shade of white as we entered the assembly hall. It was a moving experience to be part of this orderly, silent congregation that proceeded like so many angels to fill long rows of chairs and await miracles.

High on two walls perpendicular to the stage, TV monitors lit up, and we watched João perform visible surgeries. We saw him make a quick cut across a man's abdomen, pull out some tissue, and sew up the wound while the man stood still in no apparent discomfort.

"I think I'll have invisible surgery," Mara whispered. I let out a deep breath, which I had been holding without realizing it, and my shoulders relaxed in relief.

We started with an acknowledgement of our international group as we recited the Lord's Prayer in Portuguese, Spanish, English, French, and German. That done, we stood up and began to form two lines, one for newcomers and a much shorter line for those who had come to João for healing in the past. Mara was considered a second-timer because her photo had been presented to João by a California contact in November; she disappeared quickly through a door to the right of the stage.

The moment she was out of sight a hidden hot spring of emotions erupted like a geyser. I started to cry, and my heart felt as if it would explode. It seemed that I'd suppressed a tidal wave of indecipherable feelings along with grief and fear. The moment the pressure was released, a curtain of doubt was pulled aside like a change of scene in a play. What I saw next was quick yet intense, and it isn't easy to describe. In the new scene there was color and light, awe and gratitude. Suddenly, the possibility of miracles didn't seem so far-fetched after all.

The line of seekers proceeded though a series of rooms. João sat on a chair in the second room at the head of an aisle. Several hundred meditators faced him, seated in rows. Mara told me later that her interaction with João took less than 15 seconds. He scribbled some marks on a small piece of paper and handed it to her. A translator said it was a prescription for post-operative herbs and told her to come back in the afternoon for surgery.

Finally my turn came to stand before him. I was struck by his large stature and light hazel-blue eyes. It was said that his eyes changed color—

more blue or green or gold—depending on which entity was present in him. The man's appearance did nothing to settle the ambivalence that stirred within me: His long black hair seemed to have been slicked back with oil and his broad open face was offset by a hint of sinister stubble. His looming presence vacillated between promise and peril. A tingling of hope from the base of my spine met with a creeping sensation down my neck, a confounding sensation. It seemed that João revealed nothing more or less than the expectations of the beholder. I told him I needed emotional strength to support my daughter who had cancer. He said to come back in the afternoon and meditate in the "current room," which was said to be filled with healing energy currents. That afternoon when I joined hundreds of others, I practiced as though every positive thing I heard was true.

Meanwhile, Mara went into a surgery room with about 30 others who were told to close their eyes and raise their hands if they wanted visible surgery.

"My hands stayed in my lap," she told me later. "I don't know how many people left or where they went. A woman told us to put our right hand on the place we wanted healed and I touched my belly. A few minutes later she said all the surgeries were done. I didn't feel a thing."

Her group was advised to take taxis back to the *pousadas* no matter how short the walk, to rest for 24 hours, and to return in two days, no sooner. Some people may indeed have felt dizzy or disoriented. For Mara the one-minute ride in a taxi was an act of respect and hope.

During her rest, I brought Mara meals, kept her company, and meditated in the current room. When I returned from the Casa on Thursday morning, I found my sweet daughter in tears. She admitted what she had not been willing to tell me sooner: that her abdominal pain had returned the day we arrived in Brazil, and that the invisible surgery seemed to have made no difference. Her pain wasn't severe but it carried a powerful message.

Her voice wavered as she spoke. "I'm afraid it's the cancer–that the chemo isn't working." A moment after the dreaded words tumbled out of her mouth she flashed a smile that didn't reach her eyes and said, "Don't worry, I just needed a good cry."

In an act of pure will I pushed back my own tears, slowed my breathing, and regained the calm I'd felt in the current room. I curled up next to Mara and spoke silently to my heart: Soften and love, soften and love.

After her day of required rest, Mara and I mingled with other guests who told tales of miraculous cures. We grabbed onto other people's optimism like a lifeline. A Brazilian woman was diagnosed with uterine cancer at 32. She refused Western medicine, and it was her ardent belief that hope, homeopathy, and João had cured her. She said her husband was criticized fiercely by friends and family members who were sure that medical doctors offered her only chance for survival. Twenty years later she still came back to the Casa for spiritual renewal and to maintain her physical well-being.

The story, inspiring on the surface, raised many questions. On one hand, if Mara had refused chemotherapy, how would we have handled the anger and judgment of friends who believed nothing else could save her? On the other hand, did chemo ruin her chance to be healed naturally or spiritually? Was the burden of toxic poisons on top of cancer too much to overcome? If Mara could not be cured, would I be strong enough to cope with losing her? I did my best to listen without judgment and look through the lens of hope.

All the people we spoke to were kind, but here, just like anywhere else, not everyone understood our perspective. Mara later described some of the blowback in an email to friends.

I find it offensive to be asked, "So, have you thought about why you got cancer?" Luckily, I've only met a couple of people like that. While they are well-intentioned, I much prefer the company of people who don't play the self-blame game with illness, and who have a healthy balance of skepticism while cultivating openness to the unknown. I'm working like crazy to be open to all that this place has to offer.

Mara faced a big challenge in her intention to be open—the lack of any sensations during her invisible surgery. Others we met reported rushes, pains, and shocks they described "like a bolt of lightning moving through the body." Mara felt nothing.

I'm told not everyone feels something, but I'm frustrated when I keep hearing about things people felt while I felt nothing. It is a constant challenge for me to accept what is supposedly going on here. I believe some people experience miracles and are healed, and I want to believe that it's happening for me. It's hard to take such reports on faith with absolutely no sign of my own to support it. Next week I will ask for visible/physical surgery (when João actually takes a knife to you), and I hope it will help me trust what is happening here. We'll see what I do when I actually stand before him. He may not grant my request; the Entities do as they see fit.

I admit that I hoped the "entities" (or whatever they were) would see fit to deny Mara's request for João to "take a knife" to her. It seemed unlikely that she could be hypnotized by João or anyone else. In the past she had not been highly suggestible. Could it be that her intense desire to heal would make her susceptible to hypnosis in this special circumstance? My job description was clear to me: I was there for ground control and unconditional support. I stood by with love, hope, and trepidation.

Three days passed. Mara and I followed João's recommendations. We drank holy water, we doused ourselves under the sacred waterfall, we meditated in the current room, and we took our herbs. João was away from Abadiânia to do his work in other parts of Brazil from Saturday through Tuesday so we had plenty of free time. We talked with other guests, rested or read in our *pousada*, and took long walks in the rolling hills beside the Casa.

Our walks were glorious. We saw eucalyptus trees, grazing cows and horses, mica in the rocks, and thousands of tiny insects marching in formation. We guessed they were termites. Mara, with keener eyes and better powers of observation than I, noticed that the tiny creatures in the middle were orange while those flanking them were white, signaling different roles in their brief lifetimes. I flashed back to the walks we took when Mara was a little girl. Squatting low with her sturdy legs, her butt nearly touching the pavement, she'd slow me down to watch a spider wrap its prey in silk or point to an ant whose load was bigger than its bearer.

We met Toto, a homeless dog who befriended Casa guests. Toto started to come with us on walks, and he became our guardian angel. When we came to a place where more than a dozen cattle occupied the road, the only safe passage through the hills was blocked. We had been warned to stay on the path at all times to avoid poisonous snakes. Tiny Toto bravely charged and barked at the cattle until they cleared the road. I was saved from the snakes, but not from slipping on a large mound of fresh cow poop. Mara laughed as I turned the fall into a graceful yoga asana. On our way back we ran into a man in a horse-drawn cart who held out a key and asked us in Portuguese if it was ours. It was, though we had no idea we'd lost it until that moment. I managed to say *"obrigada"* well enough that he understood and smiled. The universe was taking good care of us.

Mara and I found magic in small things. We saw a double rainbow above the Casa and photographed it. We discovered that we had both brought the same book, *Life of Pi*, which we read side-by-side in bed during the hours when rain came down in buckets. We both found a passage that shed light on our experience, and I copied it into our journal.

It's not atheists who get stuck in my craw, but agnostics. Doubt is useful for a while. We must all pass through the garden of Gethsemane. If Christ played with doubt, so must we. If Christ spent an anguished night in prayer, if He burst out from the Cross, "My God, my God, why have you forsaken me?" then surely we are also permitted doubt. But we must move on. To choose doubt as a philosophy of life is akin to choosing immobility as a means of transportation.

When João returned to the Casa for the Wednesday morning session, Mara asked for visible surgery. I'm not sure if it was an act of faith, courage, or desperation.

"Not now," João said, channeling the entity, and sent her to the current room to meditate. Mara didn't comment. A mix of relief and disappointment washed through me.

Meditation was the prescription for both of us from Wednesday to Friday in our second week at the Casa. Neither of us could previously have imagined meditating two hours at a time twice a day. The environment of the current room made it possible. Hundreds of people meditated in unison while the Children of the House offered guided reflection and visualization in Portuguese and English. We were encouraged not to pray for ourselves or the one we cared most about. Instead we were asked to send love to João and "all my brothers and sisters at the Casa."

Our stay in Abadiânia ended too soon. When it was time to leave we held back: one more walk, one more lick from Toto. I began to feel that the Casa's power to heal wasn't something you could pin down. It wasn't just João, the entities, visible and invisible surgery, or the energy in the current room. It was a whole culture of love and hope.

João told Mara and me that we were "incomplete," meaning that more healing was needed. He said to come back whenever we wanted. Now, though, I had to go home and teach my students. Mara had to have her next round of chemotherapy. For me it was like leaving Neverland, and hardest of all was parting with Mara. Her life and my hope were fragile, and they could easily have slipped away.

Chapter Ten

SOGGY EUCALYPTUS LEAVES stuck to Mara's boots as she walked down the path to her house. Even after she was inside she could still smell them, pungent and medicinal. The trees in the yard blocked the sun. Somewhere between Brazil and Oakland, a light had gone out.

Mara's calendar was dominated by Kaiser appointments and chemotherapy, with four long weeks before the next scan that would show whether her third chemotherapy protocol was working. Mara had no intention of sitting around and waiting to find out. She began to think through her available options. The first choice she made was to return to Brazil during her next break from chemotherapy in early February. Even so, she still wasn't willing to let go of conventional treatment, not before she had exhausted its possibilities.

Mara cultivated her calendar like a garden, choosing each seed with care. As a matter of priority, she knew that she needed to build her relationships with medical advisors outside of Kaiser.

Mel Reinhart gave her a unique blend of curiosity and courage, a kind of daring optimism. Mel, an extreme surfer who tackles some of the most ferocious cold water waves in the Western Hemisphere, was going to ride the waves with Mara—help her stand up, hold on, and get back up when she fell. Richard Hoffman, by contrast, offered healing through acupuncture and Chinese medicine in a deeply relaxing setting. The walls of his clinic were paneled with dark wood, and old Persian carpets covered the floor. The light from a window played on a wall where posters in many languages told stories about the international healing community.

Mara's weekly calendar was also marked with names of friends who gave her a sense of continuity and normalcy. She and Lindsay meditated at a Buddhist center on Sundays and had dinner on Wednesdays. Conversation with Lindsay was Mara's link back to school and the students she missed so much. Mara, for her part, told her friend stories about her adventurous travels through both Brazil and the medical world.

On Mondays, after her acupuncture appointments, Mara often spent the afternoon with Annie. Their walking visits pleased both of them. Their favorite route was a narrow road lined with redwood trees that followed a creek to a waterfall. If Mara had the energy to stay later, they went to the houseboat for dinner.

Annie gave me clues about how Mara was holding up. "How does my girl look?" I asked her. "Does she seem depressed?" My old friend found ways to reassure me, telling me about the positive changes she saw in Mara.

"You should have heard her speak up today," Annie told me after inviting Mara to a luncheon at Berrett-Koehler, an independent publishing firm in San Francisco. The speaker had written a book about insurance malfeasance. At a table of 20 guests including the president of the firm, Mara explained her misdiagnosis. Pulling no punches, she talked about the cost-saving diagnostic test that saved Kaiser hundreds of dollars and missed her tumor by an inch, and about the all-clear report the doctor gave her when the test was over. "Your colon is healthy. Come back when you're 50."

"Mara's gaze was steady and her voice was strong," Annie said. "She told her story well—and she looked gorgeous. You could have heard a pin drop when she was through. No more invisibility for your girl. Everybody at Berrett-Koehler is sure she's going to make it."

It seemed impossible to most casual acquaintances that one so confident and clear could lose her battle with cancer.

I was 3,000 miles away, and as hard as I tried to stay level, my coping strategies were breaking down. Teaching was no longer the highlight of my days. I dreaded getting out of bed to face icy streets, a cold classroom, and students with problems I didn't want to hear. Time with loved ones, even the weekly healing circle, offered little relief. My friends asked gentle questions I wasn't ready to think about: "Have you considered a therapist to help you through this? Have you thought about home care for Mara?"

I stopped meditating. No amount of meditation could divert my obsessive thoughts. Was Mara's current treatment working? Did she have the best possible medical advice? What if medical treatments did more harm than good? Were there other options we didn't know about? Research was the one activity that kept my mind from spinning out of control. When I focused on cancer treatments, my intellect was engaged, and it kept me from being overwhelmed by worry.

I sat in front of my computer glued to the chair. When my eyes grew bleary from too much screen time, I'd let them wander around my tiny office, a converted pantry next to the kitchen. A file cabinet on my left was piled high with research papers I never had time to organize. Wedged between my desk and the opposite wall was a folded massage table, unused since Mara's diagnosis. On the wall in front of me hung a single framed picture signed M-A-R-A in perfect, even letters. The portrait of a bird was no childish blob with beak and wings, but an elegant stork decorated in six colors that never ran into each other. When Mara was five years old, someone asked her if she was going to be an artist when she grew up.

Looking up in surprise, she had said, "I am an artist."

These moments of drifting thoughts didn't last long. Soon I'd turn my attention back to the screen. I'd sit there until my back began to ache, or until my dog's cold wet nose nudged my arm. He seemed to insist that I get out of my seat and stretch, at least long enough to take him outside.

The more I learned, the more my doubts about the value of any chemotherapy escalated. According to European critics, there were huge biases in published reports of clinical trials. Positive results were much more likely to be published, the benefits of new drugs were often exaggerated, and the risks of side effects were minimized. Trials compared expensive new toxic drugs to previously approved cellular poisons. There was no evidence to show that chemotherapy extended life for most patients with advanced cancers. It seemed that Mara's aggressive treatments were not likely to help her live a day longer.

I didn't share any of this with my daughter, and I wouldn't be surprised if she held back discouraging information from me. Our open, honest, "I can say anything" conversations had ended with Mara's cancer diagnosis. It felt as though a security guard monitored our relationship, on the lookout for any bombs that might explode.

When she started the first chemotherapy protocol her chances of remission were only one in three. I knew then it was a life-and-death lottery, and all I could do was pray that Mara would be a winner. Five months and three protocols later, I hated the thought of more toxic drugs destroying her body and her will to live. Her chances for remission grew slimmer with each failed protocol. I wanted Mara to have a credible alternative to chemotherapy, beyond complementary remedies.

Richard Hoffman recommended Ukrain, a non-toxic treatment approved in Europe that might stop Mara's cancer without tearing her down. He had several patients who were doing well on it. I hoped Mel would have a positive take on Ukrain too.

Up to this point Mara's two most trusted medical advisors had agreed on every important decision about her care. Now, as Mara began running out of mainstream options, the agreement fell apart. Mel's experience with patient's using Ukrain was not positive. If CPT-11 alone wasn't working, he wanted to add Erbitux to her protocol. Erbitux (known in the popular press as "the Martha Stewart drug" because of her involvement in an insider trading scandal) was available under a special FDA program based on early evidence from clinical trials. When used in combination with CPT-11, tumors shrank in almost one fourth of patients and tumor growth was postponed by four months.

"Four months may not seem like much of an improvement," Mel said. "But that's the average. For those who respond, the difference can be huge."

My mind spun like a roulette wheel. Erbitux sounded like another gambling game with poor odds, a lottery with few winners and many more who would lose both quality of life and survival time. Still, Mel knew much more about cancer treatments than I did, and he gave Mara the best advice he could. The same could be said for Hoffman. If Mara had to choose, I had little doubt that she'd follow Mel's recommendation. He was her go-to guy, the daring doc who knew how to ride out a storm.

Please, please don't let her face that choice, I thought.

I still hoped for a miracle for Mara, a cure that left her body whole. Could John of God and the healing environment of the Casa trigger a cure? As the time approached for her return to Brazil, there were signs that Mara was open to the possibility.

"I had sharp pains in my belly last night, nothing like the old dull pain," she said. "I thought, 'this could be invisible surgery,' as I closed my eyes and relaxed. The pain went away. Maybe the entities paid me a visit." Whatever the cause, Mara's peacefulness in the midst of pain was a good thing, and I encouraged her optimism.

Please let the healing come.

Mara's dreams, too, suggested that she was becoming open to João. "I dreamed that I had a monster belly ache until I pooped out a sharp object," she said. "As soon as I saw a pen in the toilet I knew what happened. An entity must have taken over my body and swallowed the pen." In another dream João offered Mara visible surgery. "When I stood in front of him, all the fear drained out of me. I knew there would be no pain and I knew I would be cured. When I go back to the Casa, I want something tangible."

Please let it work.

I didn't know what to think. I didn't know if Mara's request for visible surgery would be granted. I didn't know if John of God had any special healing abilities or even if he could induce a placebo response. I didn't know if I believed in prayer or distance healing, even as I hoped all of these things would work. I didn't know if the culture of love and hope at the Casa was powerful enough to cure Mara. All I had was a flickering ray of hope and scary questions. What would the next scan reveal? What treatment would be offered to Mara? What would she choose? What would it do for her—or to her? As hard as I tried to be informed, resourceful, organized, focused, and calm, I felt confusion closing in around me like fog on San Francisco Bay, enveloping and obscuring my internal map of the complex terrain.

Chapter Eleven

IN EARLY FEBRUARY, a month before she turned 33, Mara was back in the serene high plains of central Brazil. She stayed at a tiny *pousada* recommended by a friend.

"What luxury," she wrote to me, in contrast to our previous accommodations. "A full length mirror, a door for the shower, a towel!"

I laughed at her excitement, but her next words made my heart sink.

"The *pousada* is quite a distance from the Casa, almost to the main road, then down a side street. It will be a guaranteed walk a couple of times a day at least." I could picture the location. The walking time was at most 15 minutes. My daughter, who had climbed mountains with 80 pounds on her back two years ago, now needed a compelling goal to go a short distance. I imagined her frail figure in white muslin, walking slowly, fueled by determination.

Mara turned down my and David's offer to go with her to the Casa on her second visit. She didn't want parental worries and doubts to cast a shadow on her experience. This time she wanted total immersion in hope.

It didn't turn out that way. Medical tests and treatments intruded, creating a divided loyalty at a critical moment.

Mara had a PET scan just before she left Oakland. From her first day at the Casa to her last, the scan was on her mind–the reading, the interpretations, the inconsistencies, the ambiguities, and the stress that accompanies uncertainty. Still, on her first day back at the Casa, she wrote to me in an upbeat frame of mind.

"No word from Dr. Wolf yet," she wrote. "I will let you know when I know. I'm glad that I'll be here when I get the news. I'll be in a position to take immediate, positive, healing action."

The next morning Mara joined the long line of people waiting to see João. Just as he had six weeks earlier, João recommended surgery for Mara in the afternoon. This time, however, Mara raised her hand for visible surgery, a brave act she hoped would increase her chance for a cure. Her request was denied. João would not perform visible surgery on anyone under 18 or over 52, in a wheelchair, or undergoing chemotherapy. "How could I have missed knowing that?" she said later. Her weeks of mental preparation seemed ill spent; her dream of a cure with visible surgery evaporated. She tried to let go of disappointment and did her best to embrace the invisible alternative.

She received and read her scan report at the internet cafe during the midday break before her invisible surgery. According to the radiologist, while all previous lesions showed improvement, there appeared to be a new lesion, an ominous sign that the cancer was spreading. Dr. Wolf wrote that the findings were "not definitive." Unlike previous reports, this one gave no information on the sizes of lesions, only changes in activity. He said that they would assess the course of the disease later, using blood tests and the next CT scan.

Mara couldn't turn off her anxiety. In spite of her "treatment" at the Casa, she had no evidence that "immediate, positive, healing action" had taken place. The scan results dominated her thoughts. She wrote back to Dr. Wolf.

> *Thanks, as always, for getting back to me. I really appreciate your taking the time to email, and wonder if your other patients make such demands on your time for email.*
>
> *I'm confused about the sizes of my lesions. I understand that PET scans*

aren't very reliable for information on size, but sizes were provided on my previous scan reports. Why not on this one, why the inconsistency?

I understand that no one test is perfect and respect your desire to look at multiple tests to determine the course of a disease. That said, I still wonder if this PET scan is unusual. From what I've heard, it would be strange for the disease to be both progressing and improving at the same time. In any case, why wait for a CT scan in mid March? Maybe I could have one sooner.

This is a terrible disease and I understand a doctor's need to be cautious about making declarations about how treatment is going. I believe strongly, though, in the power of my attitude, and I cling very strongly to all signs of hope. Feeling good about how things are going improves the quality of my life a great deal. So, I am choosing to celebrate the fact that my previous lesions appear less active. I understand that there are no promises and we can't know what the future holds, but I prefer to focus on the positive whenever I can. (If I'm disappointed later, at least I was happy for a time, not hopeless.) I wonder if you could support me in this approach and say a word or two about good things that might be happening, even if we don't know for sure yet. Any little bit of optimism helps a great deal.

The scan findings and Mara's note to Dr. Wolf hit me like a one-two punch. I knew the likely explanation for the apparent ambiguity. After a brief period when chemotherapy shrank Mara's lesions, resistant cells reasserted their cancerous invasion of her body. Dr. Wolf may have given Mara the most positive report he could manage—"a little bit of optimism"— when he stated that the results were inconclusive. Although he typically answered Mara's emails within 24 hours, he didn't answer this one at all. I imagine he just didn't know how.

Mel Reinhart, on the other hand, read the report as though it was a chart of treacherous waters, on the look out for cross-currents, hidden reefs, and concealed routes to safety. Though he acknowledged that a new lesion would mean her current protocol wasn't working, he raised a big question in Mara's favor. The new lesion was barely over the line of normalcy and might have been missed on a previous scan. He wanted a review of her previous scans by a single radiologist using consistent measurements. (His efforts to persuade Kaiser to do a review were later rejected.)

After waiting a week to hear back from Dr. Wolf, I suggested that Mara write him again. "Keep the communication simple," I said. "Ask only the most important question."

She chose to make her case for an earlier CT scan date.

I need to have some "definitive" results. The purpose for the PET scan was to find out whether my current protocol is working and make adjustments if necessary as soon as possible. Given that the protocol is based on whether the disease is progressing, it feels urgent to have the most complete and up-to-date information. I don't want to do another round of treatments on a chemo that may not be working for me.

Dr. Wolf's response was immediate. Mara's CT scan was rescheduled for two weeks earlier. I'd be with her in Oakland and would be able to accompany her to the appointment.

The scan wasn't Mara's only worry. Once again she was plagued by pain. Mel had recommended Prilosec, an ulcer medication, in January, an antidote to the side effects of chemotherapy. It had relieved her pain – and its sidekick, fear. Now the drug was no longer working. Mara did her best to keep fear at bay.

The fact that the cancer hasn't spread much helps me relax about the cause of my pain. It is more bearable if I am confident that it isn't being caused by new tumors pressing on things. I'm cultivating Reinhart's idea that it is my body healing. In any case it sucks...

On one particularly bad day she wrote:

I fear a review of my scans. I am clinging to the statement that all previous lesions appear improved, and I'm afraid that a review will reveal that information to be incorrect. Being in pain all of the time makes it difficult to stay positive and do 'the work' I'm supposed to be doing. I'm spending a lot of time alone, but not sure I'm spending it wisely. Mostly just escapist reading or feeling sorry for myself because of the pain....Can you tell I'm having a rough day? I'm sure I'll get through this funk.

I wondered whether I could get through my own funk. Sometimes anger was all that kept me from drowning in fear. Often my flashes of fury were directed toward strangers, like the young mother who screamed at her child. I sometimes offered sacrifices to an invisible arbiter, thinking, *Why couldn't she have cancer and Mara have a child? Take that person instead* of my girl. Even an elderly women tottering along with her walker could trigger my resentment and set off my ruthless bargaining. Couldn't she change places with Mara? The death of an old woman isn't a tragedy. I was shocked at my own callousness. Who am I? What have I become?

The research I had previously relied on to maintain control only added to my misery. I learned that Erbitux, the new drug Mel recommended if Mara's cancer was progressing, had been officially approved by the FDA for patients with advanced colorectal cancer four days after Mara arrived in Brazil. Now it would be standard practice to use the drug in combination with CPT-11. There seemed little doubt that this was the protocol Dr. Wolf would order for Mara. I read about the potential side effects with growing distress. The most severe consequences included low blood pressure, difficulty in breathing, lung disease, and death. The common side effects were an acne-like rash, weakness, exhaustion, nausea, vomiting, fever, diarrhea, constipation, headache, and abdominal pain. These were the risks for an average life extension of four months.

What kind of life? I asked myself. What horrors would she have to endure? I didn't want my daughter's body further destroyed by more poisons. I wanted her to have a chance for a miracle, a chance to be whole again.

I still believed the Casa might give Mara that chance. A Prime Time documentary, "Who Is John of God?", aired while Mara was away. The program focused on five people who sought healing for a variety of conditions. Although I had no idea how these particular individuals had been selected, the program as a whole seemed balanced. Medical records verified diagnoses, and Dr. Mehmet Oz, a highly respected surgeon and professor at Columbia University (who would later gain fame as a regular guest on Oprah), offered second opinions as he reviewed records and observed videos of each patient. Of the five people in the documentary, three had remarkable healing experiences. The most relevant to us was a young man who was expected to die quickly from an aggressive Stage IV inoperable brain tumor. Dr. Oz examined a follow-up MRI after invisible surgery with João. The sudden and marked shrinkage of the tumor confirmed the young man's belief that he was healing without conventional medical treatment. The success rate of these five cases was better than anything Western medicine could offer. Dr. Oz suggested that the Casa environment might activate healing mechanisms.

Mara's outlook brightened the second week she was in Brazil. She described healings she had witnessed. One was "a lovely woman [who] had been walking with difficulty aided by a cane for years. Yesterday João took the cane away from her and told her never to use it again. She has been walking fine since."

> *More importantly, Mara ended her self-imposed isolation. I met a fabulous group of people here who have taken me under their collective wing. They have been moved by my situation and have taken up my cause. They pray on my behalf, give me presents, suggest questions for João, reserve spaces for me in line so that I do not have to stand for too long, tell me inspirational stories of "miraculous" healings, etc. I expect to stay in touch with all of them.*

These people were friends and associates of the spiritual leader Ram Dass. They had accompanied him on a previous visit to the Casa. They told Mara that Ram Dass said, "John of God is the real thing. He healed my heart." They had felt the shift in their friend and the joy he now radiated.

I felt as though the forces of good and evil in the universe were in a pitched battle for Mara's life. On one hand, I could see the scan report and the approval of Erbitux as a prelude to doom. On the other hand, exciting new information and unexpected support were in progress for Mara and me, and I could see prophetic signs of a miracle.

Ram Dass represented a special generational connection between Mara and me. I read his book *Be Here Now* when I was getting divorced from David, while Mara discovered it nearly three decades later during her first round of chemotherapy. When I spotted the book on her coffee table in the fall, I suggested we rent the film *Ram Dass: Fierce Grace*, a documentary about his life leading up to and following a severe stroke. I'd seen the film soon after its release in 2002 and remembered its central message: An unwelcome challenge can be a powerful tool for spiritual transformation. As we watched together I was stunned by the side stories I'd forgotten, including untimely deaths and devastated loved ones. Parents who had lost their young daughter read a letter from Ram Dass about the way to find meaning in tragedy. Neither of us could speak when it was over. As I looked back to that time, I realized that *Fierce Grace* may have been the catalyst for the most intimate exchange Mara and I had since her diagnosis—when she admitted that she might die and I vowed to honor her spirit. But I wasn't ready to give up on her life now.

I reflected on all that had happened during Mara's stay at the Casa and the polar approaches to a cure—medical science and spiritual healing—that Mara tried to embrace. She viewed prayers, distant healing, and going to John of God as methods that couldn't hurt and might help as long as they didn't interfere with her chemotherapy. Initially, I agreed and certainly didn't want to instill doubt while treatment was in progress. Now we were at a turning point, with falling hope for a remission through the current protocol and many legitimate questions about the value of chemotherapy for advanced colon cancer. I had come through weeks of torturous inner conflict to arrive at a place where spiritual healing seemed the only path to save my daughter, but I'd not yet shared any of my findings with Mara. I had to tell her before she took another step down the path of toxic infusions.

Drawing strength from the positive outcomes in the documentary and the support Mara had received at the Casa, I spoke my truth when she called. I presented my perspective that she could be healed at the Casa, and that it was time to stop chemotherapy. I don't recall my precise words, but Mara's reply is indelibly imprinted in my mind.

"Mom, I'm not you," she said in a trembling voice. "I don't have your faith. It was hard enough for me to decide to put my trust in Reinhart's recommendations. Please don't make it any harder for me."

My heart sank. I apologized, back-pedaled, and held back my tears. In my need to see her whole again, I had lost sight of a basic conviction I held as the parent of a competent adult child—that I would always respect and support her decisions about her own life. I had lost perspective, lost my capacity to listen, lost my attunement with my daughter. I promised myself that I would never, ever do that again.

At that moment, however, I also lost my hope that Mara would be cured.

Chapter Twelve

Soon after Mara left the Casa for the second time I received an e-mail from an old friend. It was unexpected, unwelcome, and it had the potential to change everything. It pointed me to an article about a proposed MDMA-assisted psychotherapy study for advanced-stage cancer patients at the Harvard/McLean psychiatric hospital. MDMA is a psychedelic that was once used by psychotherapists to help patients cope with anxiety and depression.

"People with terminal illnesses who have taken the drug found it easier to talk to friends and families about death and other uncomfortable subjects," I read. "The benefits might include facing directly life's great challenge, to die gracefully and in peace."

I understood why my friend had sent me the article. She knew all about my own previous experience with LSD psychotherapy: the hours of spontaneous vocalization, the change in the structure of my chest, and the spiritual experience that had transformed how I thought about the relationship between mind and body. She had good reason to think that I would be open to the possibility of psychedelic therapy for Mara, but she had no idea how resistant Mara would be to any therapy explicitly intended to help end-of-life patients.

I held myself back from picking up the phone to call my friend. "Don't you understand?" I wanted to wail, "Mara only wants to live." I reminded myself that she meant well. From an outsider's point of view, it was brave and caring to offer such an idea. I took a deep breath and admitted that I wanted to know more. MDMA at Harvard? That was a shock in itself. My alma mater was still putting distance between its hallowed halls and the infamous psychedelic experiments Timothy Leary ran in the 60s.

As soon as I allowed myself to take in the information, questions rushed into my mind like water from a broken dam. Would Mara come back home to me when her treatments at Kaiser ended, or would she stay in California? What would she do to grapple with depression and anxiety? Would she be able to face her own death? At what point would she even be able to talk directly about the likelihood of death? Maybe, I thought, the day would come when Mara would want to know about psychotherapy with MDMA. I went to the little alcove where my computer sat waiting, sank into my chair, and began searching for more information.

I found MDMA in many contexts, from its history to serious research to media hype. The compound was originally synthesized in 1912. In the 70s, after LSD and most other psychedelics were made illegal, its value as a psychotherapeutic tool came to light. Therapists said the drug helped their patients develop trust, confront emotional issues, and let go of anxiety and depression. Given the public mood and politics surrounding psychedelics, clinicians worked quietly and in private, knowing that research would require FDA and DEA approval and likely push MDMA into an outlaw zone along with LSD. Inevitably, MDMA spilled out into the streets, where it was dubbed Ecstasy and its use spread like wildfire. By the mid-80s, when recreational users began showing up in emergency rooms, the legal use of MDMA for recreation or therapy was shut down.

Since it's sometimes cut with toxic drugs, illegally-acquired MDMA can be dangerous, even fatal. When MDMA (even the pure substance) is combined with alcohol or other drugs, it can lead to cardiac arrest. People with hypertension who use it are particularly at risk because it increases heart rate and blood pressure. My own fear was fueled years earlier when I watched a woman on a popular talk show claim that Ecstasy use had put holes in her brain. She displayed a brain scan image that "proved" her claim.

When the image was exposed as a hoax, the show didn't make a retraction. A Johns Hopkins researcher made news when he reported that a single dose of MDMA could cause brain damage, but there was scant coverage when his study was debunked. There was a pattern in reporting: Alarming news about MDMA always made the headlines, but when that news turned out to be misleading or wrong, the retractions were in either in small print on a back page or not printed at all.

I learned that in 2001 and 2002 clinical trials were conducted to determine the safety of doses of MDMA used for psychotherapy. To this day, no long-term negative effects have been reported in any research subjects.

MDMA is known as the gentlest, most ego-friendly of the psychedelics. It promotes feelings of love, connection, and self-examination. There are no frightening LSD-like distortions in thought and perception. According to one reporter, MDMA "brings about a state of consciousness in which it is difficult to feel anxious or depressed, or anything other than love and warmth and good will toward one's self and one's fellow humans."

I sat at the computer a long time, reading and digesting information. Finally I felt that I'd learned enough and my thoughts went back to Mara. It seemed to me that the risks for subjects in the Harvard/McLean study were worth the potential benefits. The study might well improve Mara's quality of life, if I could ever dare to tell her about it, if the moment were ever right. For now, I was simply exploring possibilities that might or might not be useful to her. If nothing else, the research made me feel better, a bit more in control of all that was flying sideways in my universe. As for a course of action, I had made a promise and I would honor it—to offer nothing that was not asked, and to take my cues from Mara.

Chapter Thirteen

I WENT TO OAKLAND to spend my February school break with Mara. The sky was overcast when my flight got in. Between rain showers there was an occasional glimmer of light, a backdrop which mirrored my hidden inner world. I was going to appreciate every moment I had with my daughter.

Mara picked me up at the airport wearing a tight smile that didn't disguise the pain that now accompanied her everywhere. We stopped at the HMO to pick up a bottle of barium in preparation for her CT scan the following day. Mara dreaded the thick chalky solution which itself caused even more abdominal pain. What a price for chemotherapy. We were back in the world of oncology and Western medicine with its ironic version of the old maxim to "first, do no harm." Dr. Wolf, a physician who seemed to have no hope for Mara's survival, was working with the only tools he had. His guideline appeared to be to use the approved quantity of poison to kill the cancer and hope it doesn't kill the patient first. I was in the position of supporting whatever collateral damage might be necessary to wage a losing war against cancer.

Mara showed me the gifts she had received from Ram Dass' friends who had taken her under their collective wing—a blue bottle with a special essence from Hawaii, a crystal pendant, poems, books—talismans of healing and reminders of the love and support Mara inspired. She wanted me to know that she hadn't given up hope. Still playing both sides of the divide, she took the herbs João prescribed, drank "holy water" from the Casa, and prayed that João would help her as she continued chemotherapy.

Mara's cat distracted her from pain while we waited for a conference call with Mel Reinhart. Izzy tore back and forth, leaving disheveled throw rugs and tufts of hair in her wake. She made spectacular leaps at a stuffed mouse that Mara dangled from a string attached to a flexible rod. She seemed to know that it was her job to make us laugh, to make us forget everything else. She put her whole self into it, and she was in mid-air when the telephone rang.

Our brief conversation with Mel focused on pain control. Since over-the-counter pills didn't help, Mel recommended Norco, a prescription narcotic. Mara was wary.

"I don't want to get addicted," she said softly. "Or put any more toxins than necessary into my body."

Mel's strong voice reassured her that the benefits were worth the risks. He told her that pain control was important to relieve her stress and allow her to live as well as possible. "Chemotherapy is probably fifty times more toxic than Norco." I shuddered at his line of reasoning.

My mind raced with questions I dared not ask: Why didn't you say that when you recommended more chemo? Why did you mention only pimples when Mara asked you about the side effects of Erbitux? My anger was fleeting, a surge of heat that faded into resignation. Mel gave Mara the best advice he could. I was thankful for his guidance.

Mara felt relief within an hour after her first dose. Although her pain began to return after five hours, an hour before she could take another pill, Norco was a huge improvement over nothing.

We slept well that night, with Izzy curled up between our two heads.

Mara was in good spirits when we went to her radiology appointment the next day. She told me she was glad that I would be with her for all of it: the barium, the scan, and the fear. What would she learn? The results would be read later that afternoon, and Mara's next round of chemotherapy would be ordered for the following day. If the protocol Dr. Wolf ordered matched Mel's recommendation, it would be easy for her to accept.

The rest of the day was ours to enjoy. We went for a gentle walk in the Oakland Hills, breathed in the scent of eucalyptus and pine, and felt the warm sun between intermittent clouds. We paused at an overlook where we could see the twin vermilion towers of the Golden Gate Bridge poking through the fog which hovered on the bay like a fleece blanket. Refreshed from our outing, we picked up free-range chicken, organic vegetables, milk, and butter at the Berkeley Bowl, a huge grocery store that features healthy foods. Mara was bored with macrobiotic fare, and she no longer believed it helped fight her cancer.

The call from the HMO came all too soon. The CT scan brought bad news. The disease was now in her liver, pancreas, and abdominal lymph nodes. Mara was to come in for her first round of a new treatment the following day. Dr. Wolf ordered the continuation of CPT-11 and the addition of Erbitux, the protocol Mel had recommended if her disease was advancing. Mara's voice was steady when she gave me the news, and in her own indomitable way, she found a positive side.

"At least there's no conflict about what I'm going to do," she sighed. The force of unsaid thoughts between us was palpable.

How could we ever have told each other everything? Evidence to the contrary went back to Mara's early childhood. Soon after she learned to write, she kept a diary hidden under her mattress. I didn't snoop, but I discovered it during a spring cleaning. The first and only page I read said, "If you read this I hate you."

Of course, I too had secrets, like my short-lived affairs. In a rare breach of discretion I once had a late-night guest in my bedroom while I assumed my seven-year-old was asleep. The next day Mara held up a glass and asked, "Which end do you put against the door when you're trying to listen to whispers on the other side?" She always had a way of letting me know what she didn't want to hear.

The first day of treatment was a full day. We spent the morning at Kaiser where gauzy curtains, comfortable recliners, and cheerful nurses contrasted with the steady drip, drip, drip of poisons flowing into the port-a-cath embedded in Mara's chest. No matter what the patient's experience, the nurses knew how to spin it into a good thing. If there were no side effects, how lucky she was; if the side effects were miserable, it could mean the drug was working. Mara felt fine as we left the Oakland medical facility and drove to her acupuncture appointment in Marin. After an hour of reclining with needles, discussing the new chemotherapy protocol with Richard Hoffman, and picking up supplements, we went for a walk, had dinner with Annie, and went home. Mara had no side effects from the new treatment. We went to sleep with a cautious sense of calm.

Over the next few days Mara got back to her routine. We took daily walks, ate healthy meals, read, watched Finding Nemo on video, and visited friends. Mara's weekly psychotherapy appointment was the only time we spent apart. It was my (and perhaps Mara's) one chance to cry. Over dinner with Lindsay at the Manzanita, Mara's favorite organic restaurant, Lindsay broached the topic of a Manzanita birthday dinner party for Mara. A tentative date was set for the first Saturday after her actual birthday, March 9th.

"If I'm feeling up to it," Mara qualified her enthusiasm.

So far, the side effects from the new chemotherapy protocol were minimal—a few tiny pimples on the right side of her nose and a diminished appetite. She joked about how the pimples made her look like a teenager again, and she brought home half her meal.

I was scheduled to leave on Sunday. We started the day with a visit from my niece, her husband, and their four-year-old daughter Mia who flew from Oregon. We sat around on the floor while Mia, who walks on her tiptoes, checked out the artifacts from Mara's travels before she settled down with the grown-ups. Mia loves to tell stories, narratives with sound effects and different voices for each character. She started with a scene in a public bathroom where a deep voice boomed from the next stall, "What's your name?" Mia giggled after she explained that the scary voice was another little girl who was just being friendly.

The bathroom stories got us on a roll. I remembered the time two-year-old Mara screamed at the top of her lungs from the bathtub. I'd only left her alone for a minute and came rushing in to see what was wrong. She had defecated in the tub and mistaken the floating stool for a baby alligator that was going to bite her. Mia rolled on the floor and begged for more. Her laughter lifted all of us, and Mara's attention stayed away from her pain. All week long, the hour preceding the next dose of Norco had been difficult. But here it was, nearly an hour after she was scheduled to take a pill, and I had to remind her. Mia was the perfect pain medicine.

Soon after the family left, Mara became nauseous, a delayed reaction to her chemotherapy four days earlier. She didn't feel up to driving me to the airport, and she asked me to spend an extra day with her. I was glad she could ask. It was the first time she felt bad enough to admit she needed my physical presence. I did what I could. I made ginger tea, left messages for anti-nausea advice from the HMO, and tried to keep her mind occupied until we escaped into sleep.

Chapter Fourteen

 **LEAVING HER WAS AGONIZING,** but staying would have been even harder. We both knew how important independence was to Mara and how much I needed my work, friends, and time alone. Luck was with us. She woke up in the morning feeling better and insisted on taking me to the airport.

As we parted, a pink bumpy rash began to form on the right side of my nose, as though I were mimicking Mara's rash. "Like daughter, like mother," she said. "Do you think you could find a better way to stay in tune?"

Back home I tried to dive back into my so-called normal everyday life. Work had a surreal quality. I taught emotional intelligence while I faced emotional challenges that seemed beyond my reach. My students read studies showing the power of hope and optimism while I had lost faith in my daughter's survival; they learned to express difficult emotions while I kept my fears to myself.

I had told my students about Mara's cancer diagnosis when I got back from Brazil. I needed to explain where I'd been for a week. I wondered what stories were being passed around, and in any case I had to prepare them for future absences. After that, they never asked me how my daughter was doing, though I assumed they were curious and concerned. At times I felt like I was on the run, just out of reach of a monster that we all pretended wasn't there. At least I could talk about my red nose and the empathy it signaled. The rash served as a visual prop that I used to introduce a longer personal narrative about empathy. It was a relief to have a safe subject related to my real life, one with a place in the classroom.

I had always had a way of physically sharing other people's experiences. When my brother Skip was seven and I was five we shared a bedroom. One night he had a frightening reaction to the phenobarbital he had been prescribed for asthma. The doctor hoped the drug would reduce his symptoms by calming his anxiety. Our bedroom curtains were printed with blackberry vines and red-winged blackbirds flying among them. It was a cheerful pattern under normal circumstances. Under the influence of the medication, Skip put his hands over his face and screamed in terror that the birds were pecking his nose. I too began to hallucinate and to protect my nose from attacks. I can still picture the birds flying at us from the curtains as our rattled mother called the doctor. He told her to stop giving my brother the phenobarbital.

In the early 80s when I first began to teach healing touch, I learned about "emotional contagion" first-hand. Sometimes I "caught" a headache or some other symptom from a student I was trying to heal. I learned to stop soaking up negative states and instead to be a generator of positive emotions, sending love and light from my heart and hands to the person I was touching. I never caught a physical symptom from a student again.

This strategy didn't work with Mara. Each time I visited her in Oakland, I acquired one of her physical symptoms: abdominal pain, numbness in my lips, now a rash. I could influence the direction of emotional contagion some of time, but not all of the time and especially not when we slept. We were happy sleeping side-by-side. If the price of comfort was the symptoms I caught, I gladly paid it.

Mara had her own strategy to manage the flow of emotions around her. She pushed away expressions of sorrow or pity and distanced herself from anyone who wasn't upbeat in her presence. When friends said they were worried about her, she got tough. There was already so much scary stuff coming at her.

"I don't need other people's worries. How come I'm the one who has to do the reassuring?" she asked with some indignation. She couldn't bear the pain her misfortune caused in others. It was hard enough to bear her own pain.

When she communicated with her wider circle of friends, she minimized hardship, let them know she was determined to get well, and asked for healing thoughts and prayers. The chilling reality was that recovery was becoming ever more unlikely, and she must have known that.

The strength of Mara's wishes kept me mute, even with my closest friends. Tottie, Jane, and Julie, who joined me every Thursday morning for our healing circle, didn't know I had given up hope for Mara's recovery. They thought I was in denial. When Annie and I spoke, I never revealed that my hope was gone, and neither did she. We played our roles of hope and encouragement and exchanged stories of heroes and everyday people who overcame impossible odds.

Lindsay bore an especially heavy burden when it came to concealing the extent of Mara's disease and suffering. After the second infusion of CPT-11 and Erbitux the acne-like rash spread to Mara's chin and forehead, and her nausea grew intense. Even so, she kept a date she'd made with Lindsay months earlier to spend a weekend at Wilbur Hot Springs, a health sanctuary in the foothills of California's coastal range. Mara spent nearly the whole time in bed and in pain. Lindsay later said it was "like going to Disneyland and being too sick to go on the rides."

The hardest part of all came after they got back. Mara grew upset when Lindsay told their colleagues at Aurora that Mara was having a hard time; it felt to her like a betrayal. Mara had to keep up her persona, her image as a strong person who was going to beat the devil. Once others knew that wasn't true, she felt, all hope would be lost.

The weekend was a tipping point for Lindsay. For the first time she believed her friend was dying, and it was unbearable. She couldn't talk to Mara, she couldn't talk to her friends, and she could hardly bear speaking honestly with herself. Like me, she felt guilty and alone with nowhere to turn.

Lindsay was doing her best to keep faith with Mara when she and Annie invited friends to Mara's birthday dinner. They had a secret plan for the occasion. Every person would bring two matching beads to represent their hope and love. The invitation said, "Each of us, in giving our bead, will tell Mara something great about her—a story or a reflection. Humor is allowed!" The beads people chose were made of golden amber, shiny metals, amethyst, rose quartz, cut glass, polished stones, and hand-painted wood. Some were homemade, some locally bought or dug up from family heirlooms, or imported from Africa, Asia, or South America. Each friend was to wear one bead while the other would become part of a bracelet for Mara. Soon everyone at Aurora was wearing a bead to display their shared symbols of hope.

When the birthday plans were first taking shape, David and I decided not to go. I had been with Mara two weeks earlier, and David planned to visit the following week. Neither of us wanted to make too big a deal out of Mara's birthday. We didn't want her to think that we feared it would be her last.

It didn't matter in the end. Mara was too sick to leave home, and the party was cancelled.

In order to manage her symptoms, Mara skipped a week of chemotherapy and began a new pain medication, Fentanyl, with a potency about eighty times that of morphine. She started with the smallest patch and doubled the dose within a week. Greater pain control meant she could drive to medical appointments, therapy, and acupuncture, prepare and eat healthy meals, and spend time out with friends. She was able to have a third infusion of CPT-11 and Erbitux a few days before her dad arrived.

David had two goals for his trip. He missed Mara terribly and wanted to spend time with her, and he was determined to find a lawyer to bring legal action against Kaiser. There were many obstacles in the search for counsel, not least of which was very few firms' willingness to take on Kaiser, whose legal pockets were deep and history of settlement offers limited. Back in October, he had poured out his frustration in a letter to Annie.

The scuttlebutt I hear about California malpractice law is not encouraging. Of course we all know that frivolous lawsuits are the primary cause of skyrocketing medical costs.

I would be beyond happy if they'd just pay for the alternative treatments we're pursuing to save Mara's life, but it ain't gonna happen.

So I'm looking for someone with a focused sense of outrage (within a multitude of outrages) and a facility to reason. An out-of-court settlement. Simple justice.

Lord, guide me through this life without committing murder.

At first I was concerned about the negative impact a lawsuit might have on Mara. I worried that it might burden her with anger and resentment, contaminate her relationship with her oncologist, and distract her from healing. Mara calmed my fears.

"I have no room for anger in my life," she said. "But dad needs an outlet for his." She was right—he had to do something to maintain a semblance of control. Neither Mara nor I thought there was half a chance that a lawsuit against Kaiser could be won in any significant way, but who knew? Maybe we would be able to win some small amount of money for non-traditional treatments or gain leverage for insisting on better-than-standard care within Kaiser.

One lawyer after another expressed interest and one after another withdrew. There were two criteria to win a lawsuit, and only one seemed possible to meet. According to California law, the plaintiff must prove that the heath care provider delivered below-standard care, and that the substandard care affected the patient's "survivability." It would have been easy to prove that the sigmoidoscopy had been the wrong diagnostic test and counted as substandard care: Mara's CT scan had showed a thickening of the colon wall in a place that any doctor should have known only a colonoscopy could have reached. However, it was very different to prove that a five-month delay in diagnosis had made a significant difference in her lifespan.

Undeterred by the responses of the attorneys he contacted in the fall, David kept trying with a new list of lawyers. He sent a remarkable omnibus letter he hoped would move one of them to dig deeper and see that justice needed to be done. Unapologetic about his refusal to own or use a computer, he made his appeal in eleven handwritten pages. It must have been a letter the likes of which most attorneys will never see, and I'm willing to bet those who read it will remember it forever.

My world right now is one of relentless pain and rage, but I assure you I am not a nut case. My roots are working-class. I am sixty years old, always considered myself street-wise, and carry all the cynicism into this situation that is the legacy of my experience. We are a family of stoics. We are not self-entitled whiners. We have never been involved in any sort of lawsuit of any kind before. Furthermore, we are in no way in denial of the gravity of

Mara's condition…We are simply pursuing the best path for her survival that presents itself each day.

Kaiser Permanente is, of course, not responsible for Mara's cancer. It happened, there it is, and I'm in a battle with God over that issue…I do not see the world in black and white terms except in the hours where the blind rage takes over.

It is the cold hard truth, and so obvious that it's difficult to write down such a banality: the decisions made around Mara's case are under the control of those to whom she is an actuarial statistic, and the sooner she dies, the better. Indeed, it cannot be otherwise under the system.

She is our only child, but only a little bit spoiled…we were fully prepared to discipline her as much as needed. In fact it never was needed; she just got it. Except for a few questionable fashion statements, a woefully underachieved attempt at Latin, and two tiny and chaste tattoos I would not have approved of, she has been a source of pure joy and pride…She possesses in abundance what I consider the three cardinal virtues: courage, kindness, and humor— and without a hint of sanctimony. She is drop-jaw street-beautiful, but that is common luck. She is beautiful through and beyond her marrow, into whatever the realm is that brings grace to our lives.

I'm dealing with the laws of man, made by man for profit, and I'm looking for an attorney who could be moved by ideals, but is cold, efficient, and vicious…It is incomprehensible to me that an expert witness cannot be found.

Finally, within days of David's arrival in Oakland, a follow-up phone call led to an appointment with a lawyer who agreed to represent Mara. With a great sense of relief, David turned his attention to having the best possible visit.

He hoped for a magical father-daughter road trip, a drive to Death Valley, where a rare bounty of winter rain had desert plants in full bloom. Such a bloom is said to occur once in a hundred years. David wanted to witness the capacity for renewal in Mara. He also wanted to go to the Ancient Bristlecone Pine Forest in the White Mountains east of the Sierra Nevada so that he and Mara could walk amongst the oldest trees on earth. The trees that survive the longest (over four thousand years), are the ones living in the harshest conditions, those rooted in alkaline, malnourished, minimally moistened soil. Among bristlecones, long life is strengthened by struggle.

It was a beautiful plan in theory, but they were in different worlds. Mara, who was still dealing with bouts of nausea and vomiting, wanted to be close to home. Instead of embarking on a grand adventure, they took local trips to some of her favorite places—the Oakland hills, Muir Woods, and Point Reyes. It seemed to David that Mara wanted to show him her world, its beauty and grandeur. He had made no secret of his disappointment when Mara pulled up roots and moved from Boston to the San Francisco Bay Area. This was her chance to let him know how right that decision had been for her.

David and Mara hung out in her apartment, playing with Izzy, doing crossword puzzles and reading side-by-side. They spent time making meals together, foods that Mara could enjoy and keep down. David said that they created "the best chicken soup on the planet and ice cream fit for the gods." One evening they went out to see *The Parrots of Telegraph Hill*, a film about an eccentric man who befriended and defended a flock of escaped parrots. It was a chance to root for the birds and their protector against the dark forces of the uncaring world.

Gentle moments for father and daughter were interspersed with reminders of harsh reality. David drove Mara to Kaiser for her fourth chemotherapy infusion, for a saline infusion when she was dehydrated from vomiting, and to pick up a disability statement. She had to document her current medical status to continue receiving California disability benefits. David said, "She broke down only once. It was after she got in the car and looked at the statement." Dr. Wolf had written that Mara wasn't able to return to work, and was not expected to do so, ever.

As soon as David left Oakland, Mara's condition plummeted. Maybe his presence had infused her with vitality that slipped away with his departure, or perhaps her small reserve of energy was depleted. By the time David's flight touched the ground in Boston, Mara was bedridden with severe nausea, unable to eat or drink. The smallest movement of her head triggered dry heaves. A Kaiser nurse began coming daily to hook her up to IV fluids. In the five weeks since Erbitux had been added to her protocol, none of the anti-nausea medications had worked. Mara was too sick to tolerate another infusion, and with that, chemotherapy came to a halt.

At the same time, her pain was becoming more difficult to manage.

Every time her Fentanyl dosage was increased to reduce pain, her nausea worsened. We prayed that as she recovered from the effects of chemotherapy we would find a way to maintain the precarious balance between Mara's excruciating pain and debilitating nausea.

Meanwhile, her friends stood by like soldiers at the ready, returning all the care they had received from her in happier years. Lindsay, on spring break from Aurora School, visited daily and enlisted others to help. When Mara couldn't bear to talk or move her head, Lindsay would turn on some of Mara's favorite music like Neil Young's *Harvest Moon,* lie next to her, and hold her hand. Sometimes they practiced tonglen, a form of Buddhist healing meditation.

"We breathed in pain and suffering, and breathed out space, openness, and love," Lindsay explained. Her devotion helped Mara expand the borders of what she could bear.

Mara told Lindsay she knew she might die, that she had already "gone to the place of death," and that she wasn't afraid for herself. She said, "I just can't wrap my mind around what my passing would do to the people I love, especially my parents."

Thanks to my friend Julie, I finally found a way to voice my despair. It wasn't because of her skill as a psychologist or the grieving den she offered when I needed to cry, but an unexpected email blunder. Julie wrote to a group of my closest supporters, but forgot to delete my name from the list of recipients.

I'm catching up on lots of messages among us tonight, and it feels like a heavy task. I talked with Marilyn last night, and was so grateful to just hang out with her, and listen, and cry and laugh. We did all of that. I worry a little about our stampeding her in any direction or in any way—as in, to nudge her towards accepting Mara's impending death. Or using our Thursday circle in any unusual way, without building it together. I get the sense that Marilyn would be wary of our communicating this way, around her but not with her.

She knew it was too late the moment her finger hit the button. She called the next morning with profuse apologies.

Instead of being upset, I was relieved. With Julie's slip I finally had permission to express the terrible thoughts I hadn't been able to say out loud—that I wondered every day how much longer Mara could keep up her fight, that I thought about her dying all the time, that I felt guilty and disloyal on top of the relentless heartache. Now I could let go of the pretense, at least with a few close friends.

"Mara wants me and everyone she knows to keep believing in her recovery, but I don't know how anymore," I admitted.

From that moment on, I gave voice to my worst fears again and again. I tried to spread it out, giving what I hoped were manageable chunks of grief to each of my closest friends—except Annie.

Annie was *in loco parentis*, my extension in California. She believed it was her job to convey optimism. When Annie slipped up with a negative thought, Mara was quick to correct her.

"She gave me the evil eye when I mentioned a sick friend who didn't want to die," Annie said, laughing because she got the evil eye often enough from her own daughter. Her own doubts were many, she told me later, but she pushed them away. Her first allegiance as she saw it wasn't to the truth but to Mara.

In April, Mara's nausea diminished. She got out of bed, ate, drank, and went to appointments. She had blood tests and a CT scan to assess the course of her disease over the past six weeks. Annie accompanied Mara to the follow-up appointment with Dr. Wolf. "I'm scared," Mara told her, "but no matter what, I'm not giving up."

Mara was prepared for bad news. She knew the odds for remission were poor and that the steady increase in her pain was not a good sign. However, there were still more options to explore, many of them provided by Mel Reinhart. By the time Mara made her follow-up appointment with Dr. Wolf, she had already decided what she would do next, no matter what the test results told her. First, she would spend a few days at the Green Center (not its real name), a holistic cancer care center in the Chicago area where she would have special blood tests and take a look at an innovative treatment option.

The following week she planned to fly to Los Angeles to see if she qualified for a vaccine trial for advanced colon cancer patients. A friend offered to meet her in Chicago, and I made plans to be with her in LA at the end of the week. There was an element of haste and danger in every plan she made, and at the same time an element of energy and adventure. Mara's ability to evaluate choices, make decisions, and take critical steps meant that she was still driving, in charge of her own destiny.

Annie accompanied Mara to the follow-up appointment with Dr. Wolf.

He shuffled into the room and avoided eye contact with Mara, focusing his attention on the computer monitor where the results of the CT scan were displayed. He pointed out masses that had doubled in size, new lesions in her liver and spleen, enlarged lymph nodes from her neck to the base of her spine, and fluid that had begun to accumulate in her abdominal cavity. He reviewed the failed chemotherapy protocols and said, "We can offer you a program known as hospice."

"I don't need that information," Mara said as she and Annie got up and left.

Mara sent me the radiology report with a note: "Ugh. Here are the results. Worse than expected, but I'm doing okay."

By the time she reached me by telephone, her humor was in full force. "Erbitux is Miracle-Gro for colon cancer," she said. "In any case, I'm glad to be done with Dr. Wolf." She didn't mention the hospice recommendation. It was Mara's official notification that she was not expected to live more than six months.

The following day Mara had an acupuncture appointment with Richard Hoffman. Once again, Annie accompanied Mara and took notes. His view of the Green Center wasn't reassuring.

"He all but told her not to go to Chicago," Annie said. "He said she has to get a commitment on a rapid turnaround time to review blood test results. They've been known to keep patients waiting for weeks, and Mara needs to be firm about this." Her condition was changing so rapidly that out-of-date tests might be irrelevant or misleading. According to Hoffman, the center had not compiled quantitative results on survival times for their patients. Instead he suggested several other options in the US, Germany, and China.

Up to this point Annie had been a silent companion in the meeting. She spoke up to express her worries about long-distance travel given Mara's limited time and energy.

"Mara gave me a major evil eye," Annie later reported. "I felt like I was in trouble with the teacher. She said, 'Ann, if I decide that the best choice is in China, I will go to China.'"

I shared Annie's concern about overseas treatments but also took Hoffman's warning about the Green Center seriously. I wanted Mara to ask for quantitative data on survival times for other patients with stage IV colon cancer, and insist on getting rapid results for any tests. The last thing she needed was tiring travel and treatment that would further diminish her quality of life without a reasonable chance for remission. However, I had promised myself to support her decisions, whatever they might be. I kept my promise, and to a large extent I gave up trying to evaluate each new option that came to light. The options were too many, the variables too complex. My illusion of control was long gone.

Chapter Fifteen

MARA HAD AN EXTRAORDINARY ABILITY to move forward in the face of uncertainty. She respected Hoffman but made a clear and reasoned decision to put her faith in Mel. He was her coach, he recommended the Green Center, and that was that. She packed clothing and pain medications for five days and planned to be back in Oakland in time for our trip to LA. Lindsay drove her to the airport, hugged her goodbye, and watched her disappear into the airport terminal.

"She was wearing her purple and blue healing colors," Lindsay told me. "Even her shoes were bright blue. She was the picture of optimism."

Mara's friend Kira took a flight from Boston to Chicago the next morning. By the time Kira got to the hotel, Mara couldn't stand up straight. Spasms radiated up and down her back, so intense that they overshadowed her abdominal pain. She had to make her way slowly and tentatively across the hotel lobby to greet Kira.

Kira and Mara had been best friends since elementary school. They had always shared their secrets and sorrows. Kira gave Mara an old TV to hide in her closet when I refused to own one. She helped Mara cope after the bad scare from our upstairs tenant by constructing crime scenes with Barbie and Ken dolls. "We'd put Stacy or Stephanie, our favorite names for a good girl character, in a dollhouse with the nasty pervert college professor," Kira told me. "Then we'd have James Bond come to the rescue. It was a game where we ruled and justice was done."

During their college years, Mara wrote long letters to Kira in lieu of keeping a diary. She shared boy crushes, girl snafus, glories, and disasters. Her nickname for Kira was "Boobs," a best-friend reference to Kira's mother-earth body. Now they lived on opposite coasts—Kira a young mother and manager of a graphic design department at a publishing company and Mara a teacher and world traveler. They had made different choices but still they walked in tandem, communicating and sharing their lives. And then Mara's path veered off course, and it now seemed to be hurtling out of control toward catastrophe.

Kira had been an anchor for Mara after her abdominal surgery the previous summer. She visited often and celebrated Mara's rapid recovery. She flew to Oakland to see Mara in the fall, spent time with her in Boston before Christmas, and spoke to her at least once a week by phone. Yet Mara never discussed her battle to control pain or her oncologist's recommendation for hospice care—and true to my daughter, I kept silent. When Kira took off to meet Mara in Chicago, she had no idea how sick Mara was.

Kira absorbed what she saw in a single glance, took a deep breath, and rallied to Mara's support. That was their way. They had practiced standing up for each other all their lives.

Soon after Kira arrived, she and Mara headed to the Green Center for Mara's initial consultation. On the way there, Mara asked Kira if she would hold her hand. They were girls from New England, close in spirit but not in physical affection. Holding hands wasn't something they did. With that simple gesture Kira understood how vulnerable Mara had become.

"Are you alright?" she asked.

"I'm scared," Mara said. "I just need a little comfort."

Mara's appointments lasted most of the day. Kira took detailed notes on her laptop and sent them to me by email in the evening. After a physical exam, a series of blood tests, and a consultation with a nutritionist, Mara met with an oncologist who had studied her medical records in advance. He addressed a whole range of issues beginning with her pain.

"You've been through most of the superstars of pain prevention," he said.

He wrote prescriptions to ease spasms and stimulate appetite. As predicted by Hoffman, he said it might take a month to get blood tests results because the samples had to be shipped overseas (in fact, it took over six weeks for them to arrive).

Most of the meeting was devoted to an explanation of the treatment plan the oncologist recommended: five more months of chemotherapy using drugs Mara had already taken without success (5-FU and Avastin). This time, however, the drugs would be administered in "far more effective ways." They would be delivered "chrono," meaning that the biological rhythms of the patient are taken into account: Infusions are timed so that the cancer-destroying capacities of the drugs peak when normal tissues are least susceptible to their toxic effects. With this protocol he said she would experience "only about one fifth of the diarrhea, nausea, and vomiting."

In order to follow the oncologist's recommendations, Mara would have to travel to the Green Center every other week for treatment that cost about $20,000 per month. So far, money for Mara's out-of-pocket expenses had not been a burden. I had a savings account to help her pay for a house some day, and it seemed right to draw from the account to save her life. Five months at the Green Center would deplete all that and more.

How much do you pay for a chance at survival? How can you tell whether the chance is big, small, or nothing at all? The questions before us now were born from desperation. Time was running out, and I wasn't convinced this place offered Mara the best possible chance at survival.

At the end of the day Mara met with Dr. Harold Green, the founder of the center. He reiterated the recommendation for chemotherapy and emphasized his multifaceted approach. According to Kira's notes:

> *He would want to start a major detox to rebuild her body for treatment...He said Mara should be doing a rehab with them no matter what (for a week). He has examples of colon cancer patients with the exact same disease in the same stage who have had miraculous results.*

When Mara called in the evening, she was excited about those miraculous results. Although I did my best to support her enthusiasm, I couldn't stop the stream of doubts and questions. What did Dr. Green mean by "patients with the exact same disease in the same stage?" Did he mean patients who had just been diagnosed with stage IV colon cancer? Or, like Mara, had they failed to respond to multiple previous chemotherapy protocols after a Stage IV diagnosis? What did he mean by miraculous? Had patients extended their lives by months? Years? What was the median survival time of his patients with a comparable prognosis? What was the longest anyone lived? Was anyone still alive? Why were there no hard statistics on survival rates? Why were there no published papers documenting the "miraculous results?" The scientist in me was going to war with the mother who, in spite of every sign to the contrary, still wanted to believe that somebody somewhere could stop the bullet headed for my daughter. We had put our faith in Mel, a respected advisor who thought the Green Center was the right way to go. Mara had decided, and who was I to question her decision now?

Had I been present in the consultation room, I probably would have held my tongue. I'm not even sure I could have asked Dr. Green my questions in private, after he had given Mara reason to hope. I doubted that any physician anywhere in the world could offer Mara the optimism she craved with documentation to support it. So I did the one thing I could: once again, I tried to have hope.

The next day Kira accompanied Mara to the center for recovery program services. She managed to get through appointments with a massage therapist, a psychotherapist trained in mind-body approaches, and a physical therapist. By the time we talked in the evening, she was in agony. All plans were now subject to change. We would not be able to keep Mara's appointment in LA at the end of the week, or even get her back to Oakland. Mara needed to get her pain under control before she went anywhere. Though with less conviction than she had going in, she said she would follow the Green Center plan, if only because she had to do something.

I flew to Chicago the next day, before Kira went back to her own husband and baby. I can still see the look in Kira's huge, liquid-brown eyes. I had known those eyes since her childhood, and they could light up a room. Now, however, they were pools of sadness. When I asked her out of Mara's earshot how she managed to stay positive, she said, "Any time I'm about to lose it, I call my mom and cry with her."

After Kira left, Mara felt well enough to check her email in the tiny guest office in the hotel lobby. She burst into tears as soon as she opened the first message. Annie had gone into high gear after I forwarded Kira's notes to her indicating that the stay in Chicago would be prolonged. She was concerned about the expense and difficulty of Mara living in a hotel while undergoing treatment, and so she used her characteristic networking strategy, a blanket email to all of our friends, to describe the situation and ask who might know someone with a room to spare near the Green Center.

Mara wasn't upset by Annie's search for free housing, although she didn't really want to stay with a stranger. It was the opening line of the email that made her cry: "Mara had a pain crisis while in Chicago with her friend Kira, following a highly informative day at the Green Center."

Mara took a moment to regain her composure and then wrote back.

While I absolutely appreciate the intention behind this email, I would prefer to communicate my situation to my friends myself. Now I have a bunch of friends that are concerned about my "pain crisis." I love you dearly and know that you love me and are just trying to do everything within your power to help me, but in the future, please check with me first before emailing my friends.

Annie poured out her apology:

I woke up thinking about my behavior and your feedback. I learned something here, or relearned it anyway. The flip side of my problem-solving skill is wicked compulsive behavior that serves no one. You helped me see that I have to step back, trust you and your journey, and go with the flow. From here on, I'm on board for your requests without inventing my own quests and solutions. You were a good friend to write as you did. Please forgive me.

The exchange was a powerful reminder of how much Mara wanted optimism and how desperate she was to stay in control of communication about her own situation.

"There was something heroic about it," Annie said later. "When Mara stood there like a soldier and defended the last thing she could control—her story to her friends."

Mara decided to begin "detox" and "build her body" (in the language of the Center) for treatment. She spent time with a yoga teacher, a physical therapist, and a psychotherapist. "This is a lot like what I was doing at home," Mara said. "Except here they seem to expect instant intimacy and it costs a whole lot more."

Between appointments, we had a brief chat with Dr. Green in the waiting room. He was warm and encouraging. His parting phrase hung in the air.

"Let's get you well," he said.

Mara expressed her doubts concisely.

"I don't know whether he's a brilliant doctor or a great salesman."

"I wonder too," I said. "Maybe he's both. I'll support whatever you want to do."

"I'm not giving up, and I don't know what else to do."

My mind reeled. The HMO focus on minimizing costs can—and in Mara's case did—lead to a misdiagnosis and less than optimal treatments. On the other hand, in a privately run facility, the financial incentive is in the opposite direction. It's hard to believe that the profit motive has no effect on doctors who recommend expensive treatments. Ironically, such a treatment plan can prolong pain and suffering with virtually no chance for a cure.

The Green Center may be as good as an integrative cancer center can be, I thought. But is it the wrong place at the wrong time for Mara? Here we were, pain increasing, money rapidly vanishing, and no place left to go.

Mara did her best to stay with the program. We left the center for our hotel carrying two large bags filled with nutritional supplements. We began to keep a four-day log of everything Mara consumed in order to assess and modify her diet for maximum health, but I gave up on record-keeping at the end of the third day. It was all I could do to get Mara to eat anything. Whenever she thought of a food she might be able to keep down, I'd rush to the Whole Foods Market a few blocks from the hotel to get it. Often she'd lost her appetite for the food by the time I got back. It was impossible for her to follow the recommendations for diet and supplements.

Most days she was too sick to go to the Center for appointments. Instead, she lay in bed obsessively digging a massage tool into the rock-hard vertical cables her back muscles had become. Although her fierce rubbing did no good, she kept it up until her arms were too sore to continue. She'd ask me to take over until I, too, ached with fatigue.

Mara added more Fentanyl patches to manage the pain, but the higher dosage inexorably worsened her nausea, constipation, and hemorrhoids. Her upper arms and chest were beginning to look like a Fentanyl patchwork quilt. Pericolace was added to her medications for the constipation. The bathroom counter and our bedroom night stand overflowed with drugs. We couldn't sleep through the night because medications were scheduled every four, six, or eight hours. I wanted Mara to come back home to Boston with me, but it was clear that she was too sick to travel. And how could I tell her? I knew what home had come to mean for Mara: I surrender, I quit, I give up.

As had so often happened before, just when we were at our wits end we came across a ray of hope. This time it came during a consultation with the oncologist on Friday. He recommended a procedure known as a celiac plexus nerve block. It is sometimes used for patients with intractable pain from abdominal cancers. The oncologist told us the procedure made a difference for three of his former patients: "Like night and day, " he said. The anesthesiologist who would do the procedure at a local hospital claimed a 90% success rate. In theory, once Mara's pain was under control, she would be able to build strength and tolerate chemotherapy.

We were going up on the familiar roller coaster ride. We talked about a future when the tides of pain and nausea no longer inundated Mara's life. Whether it was thanks to renewed optimism or a momentary lucky mix of all the drugs inside of her, the next day we got a break from misery. We strolled on the sandy shore of Lake Michigan and enjoyed the cool breeze and the rhythmic sound of the waves. We stopped at a stationery store to get a birthday card for David. Then Mara spotted a hairdresser through a salon window and made an on-the-spot decision to have him cut her hair. Based on his unusual appearance, she had an intuitive sense that he could style her hair without judgment or pity. Hidden beneath her lime green baseball cap were the long stringy remains of her once lush, wavy mane. An inch or two of thick undergrowth stood up like a crew cut. The hairdresser was a slender man with spiky bleached blond hair, a black lace shirt, leather pants, and boots with turned up toes that looked like a costume for a court jester. Mara had a feeling he knew what it was like to be different. I don't know how he did it, but with scissors, hair gel, and artistry, he made her look gorgeous.

"My new look could be the start of a turnaround in my life," Mara remarked. It dazzled me to see her smile.

There was no turnaround. The nerve block failed. The doctor suspected that the procedure offered no relief because the cancer had spread to her spine, and he ordered a bone scan. The night in the hospital that followed the bone scan was a living hell. From my cot next to her bed I watched helplessly as Mara's pain rose. Bouts of explosive diarrhea forced her to stumble between bed and bathroom. Her screams shot through me like molten lava. The nurse had no remedies to offer and was not reassuring.

She told us that irreversible diarrhea was a possible side effect of the pain block procedure. Mara's pain was worse than it had ever been, and without a bit of luck she would remain incontinent for the rest of her life.

There was some relief the next day, but Mara was at a point where it didn't take much to count as an improvement. Mara was back to the familiar suffering she had before the procedure. The diarrhea subsided, suggesting that it had been a side effect of the radioactive substance she drank for the bone scan rather than the result of a destroyed spinal nerve. The bone scan came back showing no metastasis, and she was asked to consider a second nerve block on her right side. I wasn't surprised when Mara declined.

During the four days Mara was in the hospital, the only thing that kept me sane was the hour-long walk between the hospital and the hotel. I checked mail, picked up anything Mara requested, and got some exercise, but the most compelling reason for my daily walk was the chance to scream. Most of the route was residential, with only an occasional pedestrian passing by. When I saw someone in the distance, I'd calculate how soon they'd be able to hear me and try to blend my roars with those of passing cars. With some of my tension released, I could return to Mara composed and present.

On Friday, Mara was discharged from the hospital. We took a cab back to the hotel with no idea what to do next. We relied on Mel Reinhart and had conference calls on Friday, Saturday, and Sunday. He had suggestions for diarrhea, for hydration, for pain, for nausea, for appetite, for gaining weight, and for treating Mara's cancer. He said he would consult with Dr. Green on Mara's behalf.

I was plagued with doubt and worry. What if Mara's pain never got under control? What if Mara died here? What if I got sick from all the stress, too sick to care for her? After ten days in the hotel with Mara, I needed to go home, teach my students, talk to my friends, and get back to the routines that kept me sane. The veneer of steady resolve was getting harder and harder to maintain. David agreed to take my place with Mara the following week.

Mara was becoming more muddled, less able to think straight, and less able to decide what she wanted. Worst of all, she knew it. She needed someone at her side who understood the medical options and had no financial interest in the choices. She needed me at my best. Before now I couldn't imagine that I would relinquish my patient advocate role (even to David) but I no longer trusted myself and was willing to hand over the reins. The next big decisions about pain control and treatment would take place on David's watch. He arrived in Chicago on Monday as I was preparing to leave.

I spoke with Annie on the phone shortly after returning home. "I hate my life," I moaned.

"Don't say that," she begged. "You're scaring me."

I didn't want to upset her, but there was no longer anything I could do to shield my friends from my anguish. I could no longer protect anyone but Mara from my pain, and I had begun to feel that my own death might be a great relief.

Chapter Sixteen

EVERY YEAR I REMIND MY STUDENTS of the standard emergency instructions flight attendants give passengers: "Put the oxygen mask on yourself before you try to help anyone else." Home was my oxygen mask.

Returning to Boston was the right thing to do. Mara's suffering wasn't before my eyes every waking moment, I didn't need to appear calm when I was frantic, and unacceptable choices were only one part of my daily life rather than my whole experience. I didn't have to be wide awake at midnight, four, six, and eight in the morning to keep Mara on her medication schedule. Flood gates opened, torrents of grief poured out, and I finally slept through the whole night. I began to meditate again, allowing self-judgments to flow through my mind without attachment or resistance. I let go of the sense of failure that I wasn't strong enough to stay at my daughter's side. I forgave myself for losing my balance in the eye of the storm. On good days, the skills I had learned over a lifetime helped me to pick up and move on.

I saw my doctor for a bladder infection and a rash. These weren't fleeting empathic symptoms from Mara, but flashing red lights warning of a stressed and suppressed immune system. I relied on antibiotics as a quick fix and did what I could to regain my balance.

Teaching was a source of strength that helped me rise above a sea of pain. I had missed only two days of classes since my trip to Chicago had luckily come during April vacation. It was the time of year when I held evening workshops at my home every Tuesday instead of regular classes at school. Workshops had always been a joy for me, a time to be completely engaged in guiding 25 high school students through lessons in mind-body awareness. I taught them strategies to embrace what was happening now, to let go of expectations and allow for new possibilities. I navigated through currents of grief and fear to be present for my students for three hours each week, using resources that came from the very tools I was teaching.

The evening after I returned from Chicago, my students piled into the entry hall of my home, put their shoes on low wooden shelves, hung their jackets on the curlicues of a vacant bird cage, and entered my teaching studio. I rang a bell, a gentle signal for them to quiet down and sit in a circle on the thick green carpet, an extravagance that had given comfort to my family, friends, and classes over many years. I gave instructions for an exercise that left them free to create their own ways to be together.

"I'm going to put you guys into groups, and each group is going to imagine a creature and become that creature, whether it's a monster or a baby or a microscopic bug, and you're going to do what that creature does." Soon the creatures emerged: wild beasts, a centipede that undulated and snarled around the room, a giant amoeba that engulfed a pillow and spat it out before dividing in two.

Energy was high, both theirs and mine, and now that I sensed that I was with them no part of me held back. We moved to a different kind of exercise, a guided visualization for building inner calm, focus, and trust. I was in the zone, on safe ground, far from the uncertainty of my life with Mara. I was ready to lead the main activity of the evening, a method of accelerated breathing with music.

"We are about to experience a little bit of holotropic breathwork," I explained to the class. "And you'll get just a taste of what is known as a 'non-ordinary state of consciousness.' You're not going to break through to anything buried far below the surface, but you might enter a state of consciousness you haven't experienced before, with insights that stay with you."

They chose partners and decided who would be the "breather" and who would be the "sitter" for the first round. Student pairs picked up a blanket, a pillow, and a blindfold and claimed a spot on the floor. The room looked like a pajama party with masked breathers nestled into their bedding and sitters watching over them.

I turned on music that shifted from an instrumental piece to tribal drumming. When the drumming started, I cranked up the volume. I watched a boy and a girl mirror each other's movements as if they were dancing, though they were blindfolded and yards apart. The students' laughter, wails, and long resonating sounds blended with the music. The tribal beats gave way to choral sound and meditative pieces at the very end.

When the session was over, students gathered in a circle to share their experiences. Without intending to do so, I invoked Mara by passing around a Maasai carving she had brought back from Kenya to use as a "talking stick" that gave the floor to one speaker at a time.

"Who wants to start?" I asked.

Among all those who spoke that night, I most remember Sasha, a small girl who spoke with a slight Russian accent. "At first it was upsetting to see Jeannie go though this and know that the best thing I could do was just to let her experience it. But then I started to feel like I was on a journey with her. I had tears running down my cheeks when I felt she was sad, I burst out with laughter when she did, and then I felt happy for her."

A wave of grief swept through me as I thought about my journey with Mara and the way we hid our feelings, a mixed blessing that allowed us to be strong and at the same time limited our communication. My mind returned for a moment to our goodbye in Chicago the day before, when I felt her pain and struggled not to show her my own sorrow.

Quickly I caught myself drifting away and came back to the workshop, my students, and the present moment. I hoped my momentary change in focus had gone unnoticed.

At 10:00 we stood up in our circle, placed our arms around each other, and gave a bow of gratitude for the spirit of exploration, respect, and caring we shared. Students gathered their belongings and trickled out of my house in animated conversation.

Sometimes students ask me about the origins of holotropic breathwork, and I always tell them the truth. It was developed by psychiatrist Stanislav Grof and his wife Christina to mimic the effects of psychedelic psychotherapy without using a drug. Stanislav Grof had used LSD in his practice and in clinical studies, and he was convinced of its effectiveness. In the 1970s, when the federal government stopped giving permission for psychedelic research, Grof began looking for other ways to induce non-ordinary states of consciousness. He had seen that some patients going through LSD psychotherapy spontaneously began to breathe faster as the drug wore off. They said that the fast breathing extended and deepened their experience. Based on these experiences, Grof developed his own form of therapeutic breathwork, which he called "holotropic," or "turning towards wholeness."

I neither wanted to nor could talk about the positive outcomes of psychedelic-assisted psychotherapy to my high school students. I didn't want to encourage irresponsible drug use, and I didn't want to tell them about my own experience with LSD psychotherapy as a young adult because it could easily be misunderstood as permission to do something that could be dangerous for them. Yet I knew that it had been one of the most important experiences of my life. It had to a great extent inspired me to create the Body/Mind course and cemented my commitment to educating students about the connections between body, mind, and spirit.

Chapter Seventeen

AS SOON AS THE WORKSHOP WAS OVER, my mind went back to Mara. She and David hadn't returned my messages. How bad is her pain? I wondered. How is she holding up emotionally? Is she eating? What is going on? What can I do? I felt the ache in my heart, the tension in my muscles, and the weariness in my bones, but somehow I was able to sleep most of the night.

David called Wednesday morning. On Monday Mara had been hooked up to an electrical stimulator to reduce her pain, with no effect. She had begun chemotherapy on Tuesday and just started her second day of planned infusions. She was getting 5-FU and Avastin, drugs she had tolerated reasonably well back in the fall, now timed for more effective delivery. This was supposed to be Mara's best chance for a remission since she couldn't afford to wait to begin another treatment. David said that she didn't feel up to talking to me and promised to keep me posted.

David's words hit me like a slap in the face. The last thing I had expected was more chemotherapy. I wanted to fight but instinct told me to hold back. This is not the time to question decisions that have already been made, I told myself. Be soothing, deal with it later, and keep your fear to yourself. I sent my love to Mara and said goodbye.

When I hung up, I railed at the news. What about the need to get Mara's pain under control before considering further treatment? What about getting her nausea under control? What about Mara's decline over the previous two weeks and the need to rebuild her strength? What were they thinking? How was this possible?

I wasn't at the Green Center to hear the full rationale for starting another chemotherapy protocol. I wasn't present to express my doubts or influence the decision. Even when I was with Mara, I hadn't been able to debate or resist any of the medical recommendations. Stating my objections now would only cause hurt and anger in David. Nothing I could say would stop the chemotherapy. David was doing the best he could. The last thing Mara needed was a fight between me and her dad. He was the only other person in the world who would have taken a bullet to save her.

The protocol ended on Thursday without any input from me. Mara's experience had been excruciating. She endured intense nausea and vomiting that couldn't be controlled even though all medications for nausea had been tried. She became dehydrated, and her pain got even worse.

The day before it was decided to give up on chemotherapy, there was a last ditch effort to improve her tolerance. Mara went off Fentanyl and Norco and switched to morphine. Nobody warned her that morphine might have no pain relieving effect at all. In desperate phone calls with the oncologist over a long night, David was advised to give Mara more and more oral morphine until the limit was reached, stopping only to avoid a fatal overdose. There was nothing else David could do. By then it wasn't safe to give her another pain remedy until the morphine was out of her system. She would have to wait it out. Mara spent the night writhing in pain as David sat helplessly by her side.

Thursday morning Mara went back to Norco and a higher dose of Fentanyl. Each increase resulted in more nausea and vomiting, and less energy and clarity.

The oncologist suggested an intrathecal infusion pump, a device implanted in the abdomen that delivers medication directly to the cerebral spinal fluid. Because the drugs do not circulate systemically, much smaller doses are required and side effects are reduced. Mara was told that the success rate was about 70%. An appointment was set up the following Tuesday with an anesthesiologist in Chicago.

In the meantime, Mara started on TPN, a method of intravenous feeding. The fluid was stored in plastic bags and delivered over many hours via the same port-a-cath that had been implanted back in September for chemotherapy. Because no needles had to be inserted, David could hook up and detach TPN in the hotel room.

Mara's discomfort varied greatly from day to day. Sometimes she walked to and from the hotel upright and alert, while at other times she was hunched over and in obvious distress. A hotel receptionist who watched them come and go thought David had two daughters, one healthy and one sick.

On one good day David and Mara walked to Lake Michigan and stopped at Whole Foods for a snack, which Mara managed to keep down. On one bad day she threw up and collapsed on the ground on the way back from the Green Center. When she didn't want to move David yelled at her to get up. His anger at the cancer, at the unfairness of life, at God, came out in his desperate demand. They both broke down in tears.

By the time she met with the anesthesiologist Mara's pain and vomiting were at their peak. The doctor recommended a week-long intraspinal trial with a temporary catheter that would deliver medication from an external pump into Mara's spinal fluid. If her pain was at least 50% relieved and her nausea and vomiting improved, she would have a pump inserted into her abdomen. Mara, brave and desperate in equal measure, agreed to have the catheter implanted on the spot.

At home, I listened to David's reports with helpless dread. He still hoped she'd be able to tolerate more chemotherapy once her pain was under control. I wanted to bring her home, a choice all my close friends supported. Jane was the most emphatic.

"Why is Mara living in a hotel?" she asked. "She could be at home with access to some of the best cancer and palliative care specialists in the world." The simple answer was that she was too sick to travel.

David and I had agreed to a changing of the guard the day after the catheter was implanted. Mara had now been in Chicago for three weeks and David had been with her for one of them. I took an early morning flight to Chicago and arrived at the hotel before noon.

Mara tried hard to downplay her distress as she greeted me. I tried to stifle my shock upon seeing her. She looked so small, surrounded by pumps, poles, and bags attached to plastic tubing that disappeared under the covers.

There wasn't much time to talk. David had to leave for the airport within an hour. He showed me how to change the TPN bags using sterile techniques, how to keep the tubes untangled when Mara went to the bathroom, and how to contact the round-the-clock nurse who would adjust doses of pain medication during the intraspinal trial. Mara said she'd coach me until I got the hang of the routine. It was her steady courage that kept me from being completely overwhelmed during my first hour back at the hotel.

The next seven days were a blur. The home care nurse came at all hours for crises I can barely remember: the pump broke down, the catheter was inadvertently yanked, dosages were inadequate, and different medications were tried. Once again, I was sleep-deprived and frantic. I remember Mara collapsing in my arms, unable to make it to the hotel lobby. It had come to the point where she needed a wheelchair.

I also remember a puppy. On a brief walk around the block I spotted a young woman walking her eight-week-old Vizsla, the same kind of dog we had at home. It wasn't like me to ask a stranger for a favor but I was desperate for something good to happen. I told her my daughter had terminal cancer and asked if I could smuggle the puppy up to our hotel room to distract her from pain. She could have thought I was crazy and taken off in the opposite direction, but something in my manner convinced her to be kind. We carried the pup through the lobby in a shopping bag. Mara lit up when the puppy licked her face and beamed as I rushed around to rescue clothes, plastic tubing, and bottles of medication from needle-sharp teeth.

Humor was a rare gift during that week in Chicago. Mara was taking Tigan, an anti-nausea drug in suppository form. Whether due to the Tigan or her pain medications or some drug interaction, she began saying bizarre things in her sleep. I began to make notes and read her pronouncements back to her when she awoke.

"You can use anything for a suppository—fish, cheese, anything at all," she said from her dream state. When I told her what she had said the next morning, she rolled her eyes and gave a wry smile I hadn't seen in a while.

My last memory of our final week at the Green Center was a private conversation with the oncologist. I told him I feared the possible consequences of more chemotherapy, requested some evidence that a remission was possible, and asked what he would do if Mara were his own daughter. He looked at me with a long, steady gaze, and then he said he didn't think chemo would help and that if she were his daughter, he would bring her home.

It was clear the intraspinal trial had failed. Mara's pain and nausea had not improved in spite of the nurse's best efforts and many changes in medication. She went back to Fentanyl patches and oral medications, with all their side effects. There would be no implantation of an intrathecal pump. I made an appointment with the anesthesiologist to remove the catheter the next day. Hopefully, she could infuse Mara with enough anesthesia and pain medication to fly home on a regular commercial airline. I bought tickets that would give us enough time to make it to the airport after the appointment if nothing major went wrong.

I needed help. There was no way I could manage Mara in a wheelchair along with our suitcases, backpacks, duffel bag, and box of TPN on ice. I called Jane, and she didn't miss a beat. She agreed to come on the next available flight to Chicago. She enlisted the help of my other healing-circle friends to make sure Mara would have hospice care and a hospital bed when she got home.

I made a final trip to the Green Center. I asked for and received a letter from the oncologist to show at the airport and paid the last bill. The combined cost of everything, including transportation and hotel, as well as drugs, tests, scans, consultations, and failed procedures, was over $75,000. It had been a costly four weeks in many ways. We had chosen the wrong place at the wrong time.

Mara was more than ready to come home with me, but she was crystal clear on one point: She wasn't coming home to die. "I'm not giving up," she said. She agreed to hospice care because it was the only way she could get immediate, free, 24-hour pain management.

Jane's father was a colonel, and she was a true commander's daughter. Her skills were put to use as soon as she arrived—and what a blessing they were. She couldn't get a room at our hotel when she called from Boston, but although she had made a reservation several blocks away she came directly to our hotel. Tall, slim, and fit, she marched in, made her case, and got a room. She told me later that this small victory helped quell a secret fear that she might not know what was needed or how to be effective.

The triumph in Jane's smile when she got to our room gave us a boost when we couldn't have needed it more. I was exhausted and overwhelmed, and Mara was worried that I was about to fall apart after the crisis-ridden week.

The two women had a private conversation while I briefly left the room. Jane was well aware of Mara's previous resistance to hospice care and its association with resignation to death. Jane had experienced hospice care in her own family. She said, "Hospice will take care of your mom, too."

"I know that," Mara said.

When I stepped back in the room, Mara encouraged me to go out to dinner with Jane. "I'll be fine," she said. "I'll call your cell phone if I need you."

During dinner, Jane told me that the first thing she noticed about Mara was her graciousness in the face of pain. "She welcomed me with so much warmth," Jane said, "and now I can see how carefully she's looking after you."

I told Jane all the things I couldn't say in front of Mara. "What if her pain is never controlled? What if she dies in agony? What if she asks me to help her die?" Jane reassured me that Boston has wonderful palliative care experts, that hospice would be on call 24-hours a day, and that Mara would be surrounded by loved ones. Little by little, as the wine went down, I started to feel better.

When we went back to the room, Jane packed up the four weeks of accumulated drugs, supplements, and notes that lay scattered over every surface. I organized the rest of our belongings, seven pieces of luggage in all. The only time Jane lost her composure was when she picked up a foam rubber item I had brought to keep my big toe from hurting.

"What's this?" she asked. When I told her it was a toe separator, she dropped it like a hot coal and let out a yelp. Jane could be a pillar of strength in a storm, but a toe separator came at her like a torture device, straight out of left field. Perhaps we all tend to have overblown reactions to small surprises when we're holding back big feelings to get a hard job done.

The next morning seemed like an episode of *Keystone Cops*. With Jane's help I retrieved the bags of TPN from the hotel freezer, packed them in ice, and hauled our luggage to the cab stand. Then I wheeled Mara down the elevator and out to the curb to hail a taxi.

I had a meltdown when we got to Mara's appointment to have her catheter removed, our last stop before the airport. No one was at the doctor's office and no one answered the phone. Thanks to the time difference from Boston and Chicago I reached David at home before he left for work. He told me

Mara's appointment was at a clinic across town. Our driver sped us to a huge office building with an expansive lobby. Jane took charge, commandeering a wheelchair and getting us and our luggage up the elevator to the clinic on the 14th floor. While Jane waited for Mara to have the catheter removed, I got the prescriptions she needed, filled the prescriptions at the CVS around the corner, bought an insulated picnic pack to store the TPN, returned to the office, and paid the bill. We left in plenty of time to make our flight.

As we approached Midway Airport, I pulled out the boarding passes and wailed, "Oh God, we're supposed to be at O'Hare."

I had made the same frazzled mistake the last time I left Chicago. That time I missed my flight and it was inconvenient; this time my mistake looked like a total disaster. The anesthesia that helped control Mara's pain would last only a few hours. She needed to be home and under hospice care before her pain became severe.

"Be calm," Jane said, and I complied because I could tell she wasn't kidding. As though an angel was guiding us, we got there in the nick of time, not a minute to spare.

As soon as Mara was in a wheelchair, Jane went straight to the airline counter to present the doctor's letter and ask for assistance. Meanwhile, I stood with our seven pieces of luggage. Jane came back as I politely declined help from an airport employee. Refusing help was an old, conditioned habit of autonomy and independence that defied reason at this moment. Jane vetoed my response in a crisp tone of voice, polite but not negotiable: "Yes, we'd appreciate your help."

When we made it to security we were shocked to be pulled aside for a search. We were the designated potential threats to national security, the possible hijackers, the possible suicide bombers. When Jane tried to present the doctor's letter, the security officer shook her head and said, "It doesn't matter."

"Just look at her," I pleaded as I gestured toward my frail, groggy, daughter. I explained the pain medication limitations and the consequences if we missed our plane.

"She looks alright to me," said the blank-faced woman as she patted me down.

When I saw another security person lift a bag of TPN out of its insulated pack I yelled, "Those are fragile and they cost hundreds of dollars."

"Don't touch the patient," Jane ordered.

"There's a port in her chest," I growled.

The security guard ordered me to remove Mara's shoes as she passed a wand over her body. Aided by the drugs, only Mara remained serene. She attempted to calm me and Jane with her slurred reassurance. "It's okay. They're just doing their job. A wheelchair could be a terrorist prop."

The moment the search was over, we loaded our luggage on a carrier. Fueled by adrenaline, we ran and rolled to the gate at breakneck speed. Fate was with us. People were still boarding when we arrived. The airline personnel were kind and generous. We were invited to sit in the first row of first class. We left the wrong place from the right airport at the right time.

Chapter Eighteen

MARA WAS IN A WORLD OF PAIN when the anesthesia wore off shortly into the flight. Her face was tight, her voice strained.

"How much longer?" she asked, again and again. It was as though all my plans were subject to failure without notice. I had placed the new prescriptions in a carry-on bag only to have it diverted to the baggage compartment. The drugs Mara stowed in her purse brought no relief. As we flew away from the setting sun eastward to Massachusetts, I applied an additional Fentanyl patch to a vacant spot on her arm. It was a nearly pointless remedy because it would take many hours for the drug to be absorbed through her skin, but I didn't know what else to do.

Still, time passed and the pain diminished. When we landed in Boston Mara walked the short distance from the flight to a wheelchair. She rolled along silently as Jane and I picked up our baggage and went to the car where Jane's husband Don was waiting. It was after 8 PM when we got home.

It should have been a joy, or at least a moment of comfort, to walk through the front door. No such luck—a hospice administrator was right behind us with a mountain of paperwork about patient rights and hospice policies, the very last things we wanted to think about. As soon as she left, we went to bed. There was no comfort there either, with sleep interrupted by Mara's intense back spasms and medications. By morning I was ready to collapse, but there was no time for that. We were expecting a visit from Joyce, the hospice nurse who would be Mara's main contact.

I was awed by the transformation in Mara when Joyce arrived. She literally rose to the occasion. She sat up and gazed at Joyce, and made it clear she was strong and in charge.

"I didn't come home to die," Mara said. She raised her hands and made quotation marks with her fingers as she said the words to die. "I'm not giving up. I want to get my pain and nausea under control, rebuild my strength, and go for treatment. I'm going to check out clinical trials in Boston."

With that, she got up, walked unassisted to the front hall, went up and down the first five stairs, and made her way back to the bed. She wanted to demonstrate her will and ability to get stronger.

Joyce looked on quietly, and I took in her appearance. She had a small frame, short black hair, dark brown eyes, and a smile that made me feel like a friend. She placed her hand gently on Mara's and somehow the gesture established confidence rather than the sympathy Mara didn't want and wouldn't accept.

"I'll support you in every way that I can," Joyce assured her. "I've been a nurse for 30 years. I've seen patients enter hospice care and leave it when their condition improved."

I could finally relax. I sensed that we were in good hands, hands we could trust. How long had it been since I'd been able to say that? While Joyce did the initial physical examination, I sat in a reclining chair at the foot of Mara's bed.

My 1905 home had a large room on the first floor which was originally divided into a living and dining room. It had two marble fire places, shuttered windows, and a high ceiling with decorative molding. I bought the house in 1972, just nine days before Mara was born. After David and I divorced, the two rooms became my teaching studio, and it had remained a studio for nearly three decades. The floor was big enough for 25 students to lie down on the forest green carpet for a meditation exercise. The transformation from my airy green studio to hospital setting was straight out of a nightmare or horror movie, though I was grateful to the friends who'd made it happen while I was in Chicago. They had provided a hospital bed, a recliner, a commode, and a round table for notes, medications, and a baby monitor so that I could hear Mara when I was upstairs. A bag of IV nutrition with its trail of plastic tubing was suspended from a tall floor lamp. Right above the bed a hundred-year-old chandelier hung from a floral medallion and took on its own transformation in my imagination. Now it looked like a circle of angels.

Joyce finished the physical examination and then looked carefully at Mara's prescriptions and the medication schedule I had scribbled. She shook her head.

"This is crazy," she said. "When are you supposed to sleep?"

I felt a wave of relief. With those simple words Joyce let me know that the schedule was unacceptable and temporary, and that my depletion was understandable.

She gave me a chart to record doses taken and organized the pills in a box with enough compartments to hold a week's supply—one less task to perform, one less thing I could screw up. "That's all I can do right now," she said. "We'll get you on a reasonable schedule as soon as you have a local doctor to write prescriptions. I'll see you tomorrow."

I felt so grateful, it seemed natural to hug Joyce goodbye. Mara watched our embrace with raised eyebrows and a warm smile, her way of telling Joyce it was okay to hug her too.

Over the next few days Mara progressed and declined at the same time. She drank smoothies, ate light meals, and got physically stronger. She no longer wanted IV nutrition and asked Joyce to remove the access needle to her port-a-cath. She started doing squats to build her leg muscles and on the third day home, she was able to make it upstairs to use the bathroom. She had an exercise plan that involved going up and down the stairs at least twice each day and doing up to 50 squats a day. She didn't want to arrive at her oncology appointment the following week in a wheelchair.

Meanwhile, her pain escalated and her clarity declined. Mara couldn't distinguish core pain in her abdomen from muscle spasms or nerve pain in her spine. It was difficult to decide which drug to take when her pain spiked.

When Joyce placed her hands on Mara's belly during a Reiki treatment, a form of healing touch, Mara cried out, "Please don't ever take your hands off of me."

"What makes your pain worse?" Joyce asked.

"Everything," Mara replied as tears streamed down her face. Sometimes she didn't know where she was or she saw things that weren't there. She covered her face to ward off road signs coming at her, waved away an approaching aquarium, and pointed to cowboys in the distance. Psychosis blinked on and off like a faulty light switch.

At one point that week Jane and Don came by to help us complete a Massachusetts Health Care proxy form and to witness Mara's signature naming me her health care agent. Mara listened thoughtfully as I read the document aloud and nodded her agreement until I came to the part that said, "List the limitations, if any, you wish to place on your agent's authority."

"Just don't kill me," Mara said.

I felt the ground fall out from under me. My daughter wasn't joking. I could see in her serious gaze that she was afraid to put her life in my hands. "Of course I won't, " was all I could promise.

Joyce warned me that Mara's paranoia and delusions were either the side effects of Mara's medications or the result of her tumors, which produced chemicals that could have such effects on her brain. Would her confusion disappear with a change in medications, or were the delusions irreversible and progressive? I had no way of knowing. I was desperately afraid, and it was as much as I could do in that moment to keep from screaming.

Breathe, I told myself. Jane and Don looked at me, and I could see the worry in their eyes. Just breathe. It was the kind of advice I might have given to an anxious student in a workshop in the very room where we now sat. But this was no workshop—this was life and death. I did my best to use the mind-body tools I advocated as a teacher, and to some extent they worked. At least I didn't scream.

At a time when I was too weary to do research, Joyce became my trusted confidant and my main source of medical knowledge. At my request, she pulled no punches. She spared me no information, no negative possibilities, no harsh realities. Together we decided what to tell Mara. The goal was to find a way to honor her wishes and do what was best for her. But how could I honor her wishes when she was delusional? How could I help her find peace when she wanted to fight death? I had to do the impossible, but with support from Joyce, I didn't have to do it alone.

Day after day, life wore me down. I slept little, worried always, cried seldom, and used my slight reserve of energy to complete the most essential tasks. David visited every evening after work and Mara's friends came by at odd hours, but I was the one who was always present and available. Mara didn't want anyone but me to monitor her drugs, cook her food, help her wash, or clean the commode. It seemed that Mara and I had fused. I was an instrument of my daughter's will, the part of her she could command in order to remain independent from everyone else.

Mara's friends noticed that I was tired and asked Mara if they could bring her water, adjust the air conditioner, or perform other small tasks.

"Mom will do it," she would say, ringing the bell on the table by her bed. The sound of the bell that I once heard as a pleasant chime had become a loud clang in my ears. I heard it dozens of times each day, and when we were both asleep I heard it in my dreams.

The first time I left Mara was when I went to teach the last Body/Mind class of the year. A student's kind parents offered their house because my studio was no longer an option, and David stayed with Mara while I completed my teaching obligation. Unlike previous workshops, this one didn't feel like a sweet release. My cheerful demeanor was a facade that broke down at the end of the evening. One courageous girl managed to ask me what all of my students had likely been wondering: "How is your daughter?"

My forced smile melted like a wax mask over fire. With a quavering voice I said, "She traveled to Chicago by herself last month. Last week she came home in a wheelchair with an IV." After a few moments of choked silence I managed to add, "I'm sorry, I wasn't going to do that."

My students tried to reassure me. "You've been strong all year," they said. "You get to express your feelings too. You're just doing what you've taught us to do." I didn't have the energy or the heart to tell them that I had violated my own boundaries as a teacher, that it was not their role to support me, and that this was not the right time or place for me to break down. All I wanted was to go home to Mara.

I needed the support of my closest friends, but there was no time to talk with them. No more weekly healing circle in my studio. I saw friends for a moment or two when they brought food or picked up our dog for walks. I assumed they were talking to each other, trying to think of how to help me, but I didn't know what to tell them to do.

In the midst of the chaos, a crisis intervened. As Mara left the bathroom one morning, I saw her pour some pills into her palm from a bottle I didn't recognize. When I asked her what she was doing she said, "Dad told me to take these."

She was about to swallow an entire handful of Dilaudid tablets, a potent narcotic that had been prescribed for her the previous summer after surgery. She had hallucinated her father's voice telling her to take the tablets and was about to swallow what in combination with her other medications could have been a fatal dose. I didn't need to be playing at the top of my game to get the message: Mara needed to be watched 24 hours a day. I needed help.

I don't remember who I spoke to first, but the word spread fast.

At the sound of the alarm, my friends circled the wagons and Jane took command. She asked who was willing to help with day and night shifts, recruited people for various jobs, and created a master schedule on a spreadsheet. She provided overnight caretakers with instructions—how to give medications, keep records, set the alarm, contact hospice. Beyond keeping Mara safe, the number one goal was for me to sleep through the night.

I joined a support group for loved ones of cancer patients, something Mara had urged me to do when she was still in California going to her own support group. The Wellness Community, recommended by several friends, was a place where I could share my fears and listen to nightmares that echoed my own. The side benefit to the weekly commitment was that it gave me time with the friends who drove me to and from the meeting while David was with Mara.

I began to take walks and run errands when Mara's friends visited. Although there were still some tasks, like meal preparation and help with personal hygiene, she wouldn't let anyone else do for her, she understood that my absences were important for my well-being. I separated from Mara just long enough to be helpful when I was with her. It's hard to say what helped me the most, but I was inspired by the stamina and courage of people in the support group. I still remember one comment from Wendy, a woman with a terminally ill husband and a mentally ill son who was falling apart in the wake of the father's condition.

"Some people have told me I must be the unluckiest person in the world," Wendy said. "I tell them, 'No way.' There are millions of people all over the world who suffer from war and poverty and hunger their whole lives. I've been blessed with a loving family and work I care about."

The overnight caretakers had to adjust to unpredictable situations. Sometimes Mara wanted to be left alone to sleep. Other times she wanted to be distracted or reassured. On one occasion, Julie stayed up all night with her.

"I followed her around upstairs and from bedroom to bedroom," Julie told me. "It was like Goldilocks trying to find the bed that was just right. At one point Mara broke down and begged me, 'Please believe I can beat this thing.' I didn't want to lie so I turned it around in my mind and thought about spiritual healing, and then I said, 'Yes, I believe you can heal.' And I meant it."

On another night Marty, who'd known Mara all of her life, had to keep her from wandering outside. Instead of going back to sleep after her midnight medications, Mara walked to the front hall, sat on the bottom stair, and put on her shoes.

"Where are you going?" Marty asked.

"Coolidge Corner," Mara replied, referring to a busy commercial area a mile away.

When she headed for the door, Marty blocked her way. "I don't think that's a good idea. Nothing will be open at this time."

"I have to go home."

"But you are home. Your mom is here. She's right upstairs."

"I need to talk to her."

"She's here, but she needs to sleep. She'll say hi first thing in the morning."

Whether she was convinced or just worn out from the exchange, Mara took off her shoes and went back to bed.

It seemed as though Mara saved her biggest disorientation episodes for me, like the time she said I was an impostor and ordered me out of her room. At first she thought I was her companion on a South Pacific cruise.

She took a deep breath. "Don't you love the smell of the sea?" she asked. Then she pointed at a wall. "Look at the sunset. I think that bump over there is Fiji." Moments later her eyes narrowed as she hissed, "Don't trust the social director." When she turned her head to look at me her nose was wrinkled and her mouth turned down. "You can't fool me," she said. She pointed to the ceiling and declared, "The real Marilyn Howell is up there."

I thought fast about how to respond. I reminded myself that the delusional patient wasn't the "real" Mara—a task made easier by the extreme nature of the delusion. I left the room, changed my clothes, and returned with a cheerful greeting: "Hi, sweetie."

"Hi, Mom," she responded, without any reference to the drama that had just occurred.

Mara toasted one friend with an imaginary cup saying, "Cup of tonsils and garlic? Any takers?" Her conversations were laced with non sequiturs like, "I'm not afraid of aardvarks," and "Got milk teeth?" All inhibitions seemed to fall away. Her abundant body hair, a side effect from the Erbitux, became a grand source of entertainment. She poked a hairy toe out from under the covers as if it were a tiny predator looking for prey. She plucked her eyebrows openly and incessantly to distract herself from the pain, or as she put it, "to keep the werewolf from coming out." Sometimes, humor can be found in the darkest moments.

When she was lucid she was adamant about continuing to seek a cure. She wanted a conference call with Mel Reinhart before her upcoming oncology appointment. The fiasco in Chicago left me more than a little uneasy about Mel's recommendations, but I couldn't (or didn't want to) refuse Mara. I kept silent and took notes during the call. Mel was predictably encouraging. He urged us to ask her new doctor to prescribe Lovenox, a blood thinner that had been shown to extend the life of advanced cancer patients in a recent study. Although the average life extension was only six weeks, it could be considerably longer for those who benefited most from the treatment. Mel emphasized that the drug could buy time to find other treatments, but I was no longer moved by the familiar refrain. Now it was Mara's quality of life that I cared about. Mara, however, thrived on the force of Mel's optimism, and she wanted Lovenox.

Joyce, David, and I accompanied Mara to the oncology appointment at Brigham & Women's, one of a cluster of Boston hospitals near our home. Mara's daily squats and stair-climbing enabled her to walk from David's van to the medical building, up the elevator, and into the office without assistance. We were back in a sterile, fluorescent hospital environment. We entered a small consultation room crowded with a desk and several chairs.

The nurse practitioner who greeted us was a tall woman with a cap of silver hair and a soft round face that seemed to radiate kindness. She was an expert in palliative care who would work closely with Joyce to monitor and modify Mara's medications. She asked detailed questions.

"Where exactly do you experience discomfort?"

"My abdomen and my back," Mara said as she shifted in her chair.

"Could you be more specific?" The nurse moved her hand slowly over her own belly as she said, "Here? Here? What about here? What sensations do you feel?"

Mara struggled as she mirrored the hand movements on her own body. "I'm not sure...I think maybe more on the left side...I don't know...my whole back."

"What about the intensity?" the nurse asked. "Can you give it a number on a scale of one to ten?"

"Right now?" The pain showed in Mara's eyes.

"Yes."

"All I know is it gets worse when I focus on it. Can I please lie down?" She hunched over on her chair on the verge of tears.

We had to move to the hallway because the office was too small to fit a bed. When Mara settled on her side the nurse continued her questions slowly and gently: "Does the intensity depend on the time of day? What you eat? What makes it better? What makes it worse? What positions are best? What movements are difficult?"

Mara became incoherent as the interview wore on. I helped her answer when I could, but only she could answer the last question: "Are you okay to meet the doctor now?"

Mara sobbed, "I want a doctor who believes in me, in my recovery." She had wanted so badly to appear strong and in charge when she met the doctor, but she was curled up in a ball crying when he arrived.

I don't recall what the doctor looked like. Perhaps my memory lapse reflects the way he looked at me (or didn't look at me) with a vacant glance as though I were a generic mother who couldn't accept that my daughter was dying. To me he was a generic oncologist who had become numb to the suffering of his patients and their loved ones. I might as well have been talking to a computer.

When I asked the questions Mara had requested, he was blunt and dismissive. Regarding clinical trials he said, "Here's a number you can call, but I doubt if she'll qualify." When I brought up the study on Lovenox, he shook his head and grimaced. "No point in adding unnecessary risks."

David and I helped Mara to the hospital exit. She was in too much pain to ride in his van where she would have to sit and absorb the bumps. He kissed her goodbye and mumbled as he departed, "What an asshole."

Although it was against hospice policy, Joyce drove us home. Mara, lying in the back seat, had only one comment: "I don't like the doctor."

"Don't worry, honey," I said, turning to look at her. "You won't have to deal with him."

Joyce added, "He's just someone to fulfill a legal requirement. A nurse practitioner can't prescribe meds without the authorization of an MD. The nurse is a master of pain management, and she's the one who will decide what you need."

The nurse recommended changes—big changes. She said that three of Mara's current medications were sedatives, and that the overload had rendered her unable to cope. Because it was dangerous to stop them abruptly, the drugs would be tapered off over several days. Mara would stop taking Norco and Fentanyl. Her new regimen would consist of methadone for chronic pain and additional drugs for nerve pain, nausea, and delusions. Joyce was pleased, the recommendations matching her own judgment and experience.

Only time would tell what we could hope for now. For me it had become stark and simple: I wanted Mara out of pain and I wanted the daughter I had known to come back.

Chapter Nineteen

IT WAS THE WORST OF TIMES, and the circle of friends that stepped up to help could not have been more generous, caring, and able. The beauty of it was that we were surrounded by support that never failed. The horror of it was that we were surrounded by support that never left.

The people who stood by us came from next door and from 3,000 miles away, from recent acquaintances to people Mara had known all her life.

By the time we'd been home for a week, bouquets of flowers and cards covered every table and ledge in the studio-turned-hospital room, gifts from across the country piled up in the corners, and home-cooked meals filled the refrigerator and freezer.

I was grateful beyond words, but at the same time I reeled from the obliteration of the privacy, solitude, and former simplicity of my home. I was helpless to stop the progression of Mara's disease, and now I felt equally helpless to control my sanctuary, as though I was being violated by too much kindness. The front door was left unlocked, and friends and neighbors came and went all day long. There wasn't enough room in the freezer for the food they brought. Each time my frustration threatened to overtake my appreciation, I struggled to suppress the ungrateful thoughts and felt ashamed.

Our friends were sensitive to my conflicting emotions. Some expressed their concern about intruding, but they still showed up to help. Others worried that their discomfort would show or that they would say or do the wrong thing. Although Mara and I were close to everyone who came, many of our friends didn't know each other. Those who were most aware of our need for peace and quiet tried to set boundaries for others who, in turn, resented their efforts.

Annie had known us all Mara's life but she had left for the West Coast fifteen years ago, and by now we had only a few friends in common. It was hard for Annie to fly back to see Mara. Her father had just died, she was exhausted, and she had a lingering cough.

The night Annie arrived, all hell broke loose. She coughed loud enough for Mara to cover her ears in the bedroom below. The person on overnight watch gave Mara methadone four hours early, a potential overdose. Early the next morning a nurse at hospice instructed me to call an ambulance. By the time the wailing siren announced its arrival, I was scrambling to get us ready to go, and Annie was looking on with a gaze so mournful that Mara, protective of her image even in the face of death, turned away.

Jane stopped by just after Mara and I left in the ambulance. Annie, sitting outside on the front stairs, wouldn't tell her what hospital we went to. Both of them wanted to help. Jane's daughter was a medical resident who might have checked on us. Annie believed she was protecting my privacy. I could picture my two dear friends locking eyes, and I could feel the tension between them. Annie quickly sensed it was time for her to go home.

She rescheduled her return flight after only one more day. When David came to pick her up, she stood outside the door of the room and said goodbye to Mara from a distance.

"Can't come any closer with this wicked cough," she said with a half smile, but it wasn't the real reason. Mara absolutely did not want an emotional good-bye—not from Annie, not from anyone. The potential meaning of good-bye had become unbearable. Mara held the line with courage and dignity.

"Bye, Annie. See you in California," she said, as though at the end of an ordinary visit. I stood in the doorway and watched Annie and David drive away.

Annie wrote me a note while she waited for her flight:

Sitting here at the airport I feel so sad and my ribs hurt from coughing. Better judgment would have been to stay home, if only because I was tired and had an uneasy sense of too many people in the mix. My time to help was when Mara was in California.

Much later, Annie put her experience in the larger context of the challenges close friends and family face when someone they love is very sick. She wrote:

You want to do something. For a while, your actions seem to be (or actually are) helpful. The intention to help is half ego, because you feel pleased with your connections and contributions – and the other half is love. You love the person so much, and you want to be part of the miracle you pray for. Even if there is no miracle, you want to demonstrate your love in word and deed. In time, things worsen, and the one you love needs to be surrounded by her very closest people, the family circle. You don't understand this and you keep doing more to help. People form a team and they come and go from the family's home all day long, and make food that jams the freezer, all with best intentions. It's getting chaotic, going downhill fast.

It is so hard to make the turn. To understand that "in letting go it all gets done; when you try and try, the world is then beyond winning." That's a quote from Lao Tzu that might as well be written on my gravestone. You feel angry at yourself, and angry at God, and you might externalize that anger, getting angry with someone else who reminds you of yourself trying too hard to help. It takes a long time to let go.

I had played my own role in the chaos. I wasn't able to articulate boundaries to help friends make the best decisions. I had known that Annie was exhausted, that she had a cough, and that it would be hard to cope with one more friend under my roof. Despite it all, I never told her not to come.

The week of turmoil made it clear to me that I had to take charge of my home and my daughter's care. When Mara nearly overdosed herself, I thought I had to give up control. I knew I couldn't keep watch every minute, 24 hours a day, and I couldn't count on myself to do everything right. Yet in the last week, with too many helpers, Mara was nearly overdosed by one of the very people who had come to help keep her safe. Mara's watchful friends couldn't guarantee Mara's safety any more than I could.

I knew that no one else could set boundaries for me. I started to make clear what help I needed, when, and from whom. For example, I figured out that one thing I definitely needed was transportation. I hadn't owned a car in 30 years and was proud of my choice to travel by bike or public transportation, but things were different now. Time was of the essence, and besides, it was good to have companionship during my brief periods away from Mara.

Our friends understood the changing situation and respected my wishes. I had a feeling they were as relieved as I was.

As it turned out, I needed less help after Mara adjusted to the new medications. Her pain and nausea were under better control, and her hallucinations subsided, telling us that they had not been the result of the cancer after all. As she was weaned from her old medications, her sharp mind returned.

Chapter Twenty

SANITY IS A MIXED BLESSING when it means knowing that life will end soon. When Mara's mental clarity returned, so too did her single-minded quest to be rid of the terrifying beast in her body.

Once again she endured the scans. Though she detested them, she saw them as a necessary way to decide on future treatments. The oncologist, however, seemed to have ordered them for a different reason—to help Mara come to grips with the reality of her illness.

Unfortunately, accepting the reality of her illness was still the last thing Mara wanted.

We were waiting for a routine visit from Joyce on the day the scan report was due. I was slumped on the chair by Mara's bed gazing at alternating streaks of light and shadow that filtered through the wooden shutters. They stretched across the green rug, crept up the bottom of the recliner and projected striped stockings on my bare feet.

When Joyce arrived Mara was in her hospital bed sipping a smoothie. Mara gave a half smile, sat up against the pillows, and her face turned serious. "I don't want to know the scan results," she said. "Please don't tell me."

"Whatever you wish," Joyce said. Her serious expression matched Mara's.

In the past Mara had wanted to see scan reports right away, and we would use them as maps for healing visualizations. Did the change signal Mara's deepening denial of her illness, or was it her way of saying that she knew the results were bad? Was she afraid that more bad news would destroy her last sliver of hope? Did she believe that miracles were only granted to those who never gave up?

What was certain was that in refusing to see the results, Mara was exercising the only real control she had left.

"What about me?" I asked her. "Do you want me to know the results?"

Mara's silence, along with her slightly raised eyebrows and pinched lips, conveyed what she couldn't tell me directly: "Pretend you don't know."

"If you don't want to see the report, I don't either," I said. "As long as your medical team has all the information, I don't need to look at it."

Mara's face relaxed, and I felt a wave of relief.

I kept my word, at least literally. I didn't look at the report. But when Joyce called later in the day with news of the results I asked her to tell me the gist of it.

"Not good," she said. Mara's cancer had spread from all previous locations and was now growing in her lungs as well.

I was prepared for the news, but being prepared did nothing to prevent the searing pain that came along with it. Not at all, but I pushed away the grief and kept the monster in the closet. All I could do was continue to carry out Mara's requests for treatment.

We made an appointment at the Dana Farber Cancer Institute (located next to Brigham & Women's) to discuss clinical trials with the head research doctor. Mara struggled to sit up through the appointment, trying to look like someone who might beat the odds. The doctor told us that the only trial available for entry involved long days of infusions at the clinic and frequent testing.

"You can apply if you wish," he told us. "But you should know that participants rarely benefit. They do a great service for science and for future patients." She decided not to apply for the trial.

Mel Reinhart had one rabbit left to pull out of his hat. He told us the results of a clinical trial for Tarceva, a brand-new therapy for advanced colon cancer. According to Mel, the drug slowed disease progression in 30% of the patients, and came in tablets so Mara could take it at home. Tarceva was the last mainstream medical option available, and Mara wanted to give it a shot. The trial started a week later, and it felt good to have made the decision to try a new course of action.

Mara had to discontinue the drug after three days. It had caused her to double over from intense cramps and writhe as diarrhea exploded through her cancer-ridden abdomen.

"I want to die!" she cried, over and over.

I sat by her side repeating, "This will pass." But I couldn't stop the thought: *I want to go with you.*

Within a few days Mara's pain returned to where it had been before the Tarceva trial. She no longer asked for contact with Mel Reinhart, and I was relieved. He had been a source of hope until she got sicker, when his recommendations (in particular the Chicago treatments) had begun to have huge costs and consequences of their own.

David, on the other hand, continued to see Mel as Mara's last best hope for survival and began his own phone consultations with him. I didn't object. We had other resources now, and I knew we'd never follow another one of his suggestions. On the other hand, Mel became a lifeline at a time when David was running out of energy. Up to now, David's pursuit of legal action had given him something to focus on. It had been a way to do something for Mara, a set of tasks to counteract his feelings of helplessness, and a means to channel his anger before it built up to destructive rage. It had taken him countless hours over many months to find a lawyer to represent Mara and prepare materials for the case. Successful litigation depended on finding an oncologist willing to testify that Mara's misdiagnosis and the five-month delay in treatment had made a difference in her lifespan. The oncologist who was lined up backed out of the commitment a week before the arbitration hearing was to take place, and Mara's attorney withdrew from the case. David was desperate, and consultations with Mel seemed to keep him afloat. Perhaps Reinhart's ideas gave David the same burst of energy they once gave Mara. We were all desperate, each in our own way, grabbing for whatever it took to stay strong.

On a day when Mara's pain was at its height, she had a private conversation with Joyce at her bedside. It was mid-June, a month since Mara entered hospice care. She told Joyce that she wasn't afraid to die, but that she couldn't bear to think about what her death would do to her parents.

Joyce waited for Mara to drift off before joining me in the kitchen.

When I saw the concern in her gaze, I stopped chopping vegetables and invited her to sit down at the table. She told me what Mara had said.

"Oh, God. That's what she told me months ago," I said. "I tried to reassure her." It was a good thing I put down the knife because I was trembling.

Joyce put her hand on mine. "I think the reason Mara's pain is so hard to control is that she's getting something out of it. Her focus on physical pain keeps her mind off deeper emotional suffering. She doesn't want to face your despair."

Her insight tore me apart, and later that evening I tried to give Mara permission to let go.

"Are you fighting so hard for me and your dad?" I asked as gently as I could.

"No!" she cried in a flash of fury. "I'm fighting for me." I had touched her most vulnerable nerve, and she made it clear that she would not be comforted. I had to respect her will and her anger. She wasn't going to change her mind. "This is not about you, and I won't quit."

Pain was all around us, offset only by my daughter's obsessive courage. Obsession and courage—she had both qualities. Whether in spite of the pain or because of it, Mara kept up her 50 squats a day, trudged up and down stairs, and, one afternoon at the end of May, she walked around the block with her dad.

She asked me to keep searching for alternative cures, whatever I could find. She had stopped chewing the bitter pills she'd gotten from the Tibetan healer in the fall because the taste made her nauseous. Now I ground up three kinds of hard, hand-rolled pills with a mortar and pestle, put them into gel caps, and gave them to her with each meal. My days were spent looking after her and doing precisely as she asked.

The regimen Mara followed had taken on an obsessive quality. Nothing could be microwaved, heated in aluminum cookware, or stored in plastic containers unless the food was cooled. All her food had to be organic. I never questioned Mara's reasoning or cut corners, but my diligence wasn't only for her sake. The ritual itself was comforting, a complex, repetitive set of activities I carried out mindfully to keep at bay the wave of helplessness that threatened to wash me away.

I found alternative healers who were willing to make house calls—an

acupuncturist, a massage therapist, and a Feldenkrais practitioner. Our
family chiropractor came three days a week during his lunch break to
adjust Mara's spine, provide a tender touch, and make her smile at his wry
humor. He refused to be paid.

One request Mara made of me was harder than the others—to guide
her through cancer-fighting visualizations. The first time she had asked
she was still in California and I was there on a visit. She wanted to study
her scan reports, look at photographs and diagrams of the liver, pancreas,
lymph nodes, cancer cells, and immune cells, understand how killer cells
and macrophages work, and turn that knowledge into an imaginative lens.
In those early days, I was glad to help her dissolve lesions in her mind's eye.
Now it was a more desperate time and place. Cancer was rapidly taking over
her body and, given her instruction to be held ignorant of her scan results,
I had to skip over the lesions she didn't want to know about. Even if I could
have been honest with her, focusing on the cancer seemed to increase both
her pain and my own sense of futility. I was like a soldier going into battle
to demonstrate loyalty, knowing that there was no way to win.

Did I take after Mara or did she take after me? I was in a different
place on the path to acceptance, but I marched along as willfully as my
daughter. Every ounce of my being kept saying: Don't quit. But I did find
ways to create moments of calm. I decided to begin the visualizations with
a relaxation phase using skills I had cultivated for over twenty years as a
teacher—a trance-inducing tone of voice, a hypnotic cadence, and peaceful
imagery. I gradually extended the exercises and kept Mara's mind focused
on the healthy parts of her body in increasing detail:

> *Let your eyelids close so very gently…*
> *like butterflies alighting…*
> *too tired to move again…*
> *Feel your eyes sink deep, deep down*
> *toward the back of your head…*
> *through cool soothing liquid…*
> *resting quietly…*
> *Now bring your awareness to your forehead…*
> *Feel how wide…*
> *and smooth…*
> *and soft it can be…*

Let your eyebrows slide away from each other
Easing gently toward your ears...
Feel the softened place between your brows...
How soothed it is...

Many times, Mara had fallen asleep by the time I was done. My skills successfully soothed her. My whole life, it seemed, had been preparing me to be present for my daughter in this moment.

Chapter Twenty-One

CHARTREUSE LEAVES DEEPENED to summer green, the pastel carpet of fallen blossoms blew away, and the aroma of basil and mint from urban gardens replaced the sweet scent of lilacs. The season of renewal and hope was nearly gone.

Mara had now been home for five weeks, and her pain was once again spiraling out of control. Huge increases in her methadone dose gave no relief. A deep ache throbbed through her left side, the only side she could bear to lie on. The nights were worse than the days, and Mara began asking me to guide her through visualizations every time she woke up. To avoid getting completely exhausted, I began to record the visualization exercises. Mara played them over and over to distract her from the pain and loneliness of the long nights.

Like cascading dominoes, one problem led to another. It was as hard for Mara to stay awake during the day as it was for her to sleep at night. She was perpetually exhausted from sleep loss and groggy from medication.

Sporadic heart palpitations triggered fear which in turn amplified her pain. The palpitations were a warning sign that her methadone dose was reaching its limit. There is a point beyond which the dose cannot go, when the medication kills the patient. Joyce was at her wit's end, and the palliative care experts she consulted had no plan for what to do next.

Just when hope was almost gone, my thoughts returned to an option I hadn't dared discuss with Mara earlier. I dug up the article I had saved about the proposed MDMA-assisted psychotherapy study for advanced-stage cancer patients at Harvard/McLean Psychiatric Hospital. The aim of the clinical trial was to find out whether MDMA could help terminal cancer patients come to grips with end-of-life anxiety and depression and overcome their suffering. I reread the article with heightened interest, particularly the quote that "people with terminal illnesses who have taken the drug found it easier to talk to friends and families about death and other uncomfortable subjects...The benefits might include facing directly life's great challenge, to die gracefully and in peace."

I wasn't about to dive into uncharted waters without Joyce's support. I showed her the article, and she shared my enthusiasm. Within a couple of days she contacted the psychiatrist in charge of the clinical trial and reported back. "The study sounds like it was made-to-order for Mara, and the doc said he'd be glad to speak with you."

First I had to discuss the proposed trial with Mara, a task I approached with trepidation. As expected, as soon as I began to tell her about the study, she snapped.

"I'm not interested in discussing end-of-life issues. Who told you about this? How could they be so insensitive?"

Instead of answering questions, I said, "There's another way to look at the trial. What if the study supports the individual goals of the patients? What if you had a spiritual experience? What if you tapped into a transcendent source of healing?"

Mara's expression changed from anger to interest. She knew psychedelics could trigger transcendent states. She hadn't forgotten the dialogue about drugs we'd had when she was in high school. If psychedelic psychotherapy could induce a mystical experience and healing for me, perhaps it could do the same for her. She asked me to find out more about the McLean study.

With the clinical trial, it felt as if we had a fighting chance for a treatment to address Mara's emotional distress and mounting pain. MDMA-assisted psychotherapy seemed like a godsend, an option that could support both Mara's expressed intention to heal and my unexpressed wish that if her death came soon it would be a good one.

My conversation with the McLean psychiatrist ended in profound disappointment. The doctor was warm, down to earth, and forthright. Yes, Mara was exactly the kind of patient he hoped to help; yes, she deserved to have her goals respected; and yes, the researchers would support her wishes if she were a subject. The study, however, was not ready to enroll patients yet. Although the FDA had approved the trial over a year earlier, the Drug Enforcement Administration was still trapped in its suspicion of MDMA and continued to block the study with one bureaucratic hurdle after another. It was highly unlikely that the trial would be available in time for my daughter.

"I wish your daughter could be our first subject," the doctor told me. "I'm very sorry. I can't help her."

I railed at the war on drugs and its cruel consequences—promising research blocked, patients denied medicines that could relieve suffering, prisons overflowing with non-violent felons in need of treatment, and resources wasted on an endless war that multiplies the problems it is supposed to solve. The war on drugs seemed like a monstrous caricature of addiction, an endless drive for a fix that never fixes anything.

The helplessness I felt watching my daughter suffer now turned to anger. I'd be damned if legal limitations or the threat of consequences would stop me from helping Mara. My straight-edge daughter cheered me on. She encouraged me as I contacted everyone I knew who might lead us to a psychedelic therapist.

Within a week, I found Allan. He told me over the phone that he had a great deal of experience sitting for people during psychedelic sessions, and he was convinced of their therapeutic value. He was touched by Mara's situation and willing to meet with me. He would be in the Boston area frequently in the coming months. We both wanted to know more about each other before deciding whether it was appropriate for him to work with Mara. Mara was thrilled that I'd found a possible therapist and was willing to trust my judgment.

Allan and I met in person the next day. We spent nearly two hours discussing our backgrounds, Mara's living situation, her physical and emotional state, her medications, and her goals for therapy. We shared our frustration that research on the positive uses of psychedelics had been banned for decades and that we were forced to meet in secret in order to plan a crime of compassion. Allan was reassured by my knowledge and experience, the privacy of my home environment, the support of the hospice nurse, and our strong support system. I, in turn, was impressed by Allan's comprehensive knowledge of psychedelics, his awareness of the medical risks, his access to pure psychedelic drugs, and his offer to give Mara his time and the MDMA free of charge. I was convinced that he was the right person to work with her. He asked if I would be the co-therapist for the sessions to provide Mara with a male-female team and the greatest possible sense of safety and support. I was more than willing.

Once the decision was made, we discussed how to proceed. Our guiding principle was to minimize the risks and optimize the benefits of psychedelic therapy. We would be careful not to compromise Mara's palliative care in any way. Rather than interrupt her conventional treatments, MDMA would be administered on top of her other medications. One disadvantage of this approach was that methadone could dampen the effects of the MDMA and require us to use a higher dose of the drug. Of greater concern were the unpredictable interactions of the eight drugs Mara was currently taking and the risk of adding yet another unknown variable to the mix. Would MDMA be the final straw, pushing her system beyond what it could handle and overwhelming her dwindling physical and emotional reserves? Palliative care is a fine art in which the risk of death from medications is often weighed against the potential to relieve suffering.

Allan and I tried to calculate the odds of adding MDMA to an already dangerous mix. Because the drug increases heart rate and blood pressure, it would add a small risk of heart attack, but that risk seemed far less dangerous than continuing to accelerate her dosage of methadone. Only Joyce's daily monitoring of Mara's vital signs could guard against potential overdoses and fatal interactions under her current regimen. I couldn't legally ask Joyce to be present for the MDMA session, but in her place I could take Mara's blood pressure and pulse while she was under the effects of the drug. Allan and I could assess the effect of an initial moderate dose of the psychedelic to determine if it was safe to give her more. Allan agreed to consult a physician with expertise in drug interactions who would review the risks. He would call me as soon as he was satisfied that we should proceed.

For the sake of Allan's privacy and security, I can't describe many important details about his role in Mara's care—such as our meeting place, his professional background, the colleagues he consulted on drug interactions, how he acquired pure psychedelic drugs, and what motivated him to jeopardize his career and risk legal consequences to help Mara. Yet all of these factors were crucial to our decision to go forward with the MDMA therapy.

After the meeting with Allan, my mind raced. Would Mara trust Allan as much as I did? What would David's reaction be? Could MDMA therapy be the answer to Mara's uncontrollable pain? What if something went terribly wrong? Slow down. Breathe. Don't let fear get in the way. Give Mara this chance.

By the time I got home I was ready to tell my daughter what I had learned about Allan and recommend that she go ahead with psychedelic therapy.

Mara hadn't spoken on the phone with Lindsay or any of her other friends during the six weeks she'd been under hospice care. Soon after we got home from Chicago, she handed me a note with Lindsay's telephone number and the message, "Tell her I'm okay. Spread the word."

I thought Mara was out of earshot when I called Lindsay. I tried to be upbeat as I described the wonderful hospice nurse and our hopes for better pain management. I wanted to respect Mara's wishes, but I couldn't lie. Rather than tell her Mara was okay, I said, "She wants you to spread the word that she's okay."

In the background I heard Mara start to cry. "Tell her I didn't come home to die," she called out. When I checked on Mara after the phone call she had regained her composure and asked only to hear what Lindsay had said.

Lindsay came to visit as soon as the school year was over. She arrived from California early in the morning on the same day I met Allan. Mara made her way unsteadily to the front hall as I hugged Lindsay at the door. Mara's smile of welcome didn't hide the newly exposed angle of her jaw, her cheek bones underscored by shadows, or her sunken eyes. Lindsay was stunned.

When Joyce came for her morning visit, Lindsay took a private moment with her in the kitchen to ask the question she could no longer avoid.

"Is she going to die soon?"

"Most likely."

"Does Mara know?"

"She doesn't want to."

After Joyce left, I said something in front of Mara and Lindsay that I regretted the moment the words left my lips. I wondered aloud where my student workshops would take place in the fall since my teaching studio was now a hospital room.

"Mom, I'm going to be back in Oakland by then," Mara said, using the opportunity to let Lindsay know she was only willing to talk about a positive future. Lindsay worried that Mara's refusal to talk about her impending death added to her misery, but she didn't dare challenge her. She knew she had to follow Mara's lead or the friendship would die before the friend.

If truth and candor were sacrificed, it was worth the price. Lindsay's four-day visit was a blessing for us all. Mara was happy in her company, and I knew she was safe in Lindsay's care. Lindsay entertained her with stories from school, they laughed over David Sedaris stories, and they challenged each other with games of Boggle.

During one brief exchange in the kitchen Lindsay said to me, "I still can't beat her at Boggle. How can she be so sharp and so sick at the same time?"

"I've wondered the same thing," I said. "A couple of days ago David and I challenged her to a three-way game. She skunked both of us."

It felt good to talk about Mara's victories.

Besides the pleasure of her company, Lindsay's visit gave me time to run errands, go for dog walks in the woods, and even squeeze in a couple of workouts. Life felt a bit more normal. I felt as though we were expanding the borders of what we could bear.

Lindsay entered the scene with fresh eyes and saw things that Mara and I had overlooked, things that could change in spite of all that could not. She noticed what we had stopped seeing: the clinical look of the adjustable bed, the exposed commode, and the large round bedside table overflowing with medications. Soon after I returned home from my appointment with Allan, Lindsay went on a mission to beautify Mara's environment before the first psychedelic session.

She bought a blue and green plaid cloth to cover the commode and a circular tablecloth embroidered with a delicate floral design to drape over the bedside table. She consolidated Mara's medications on shelves to the right of her bed. She cleared the mantle to display an exquisite arrangement of purple flowers from the Aurora families, and carefully arranged student-made crafts, votive candles, crystals, carved stones, and colorful beads around a statue of Ganesh, the elephant-headed Hindu god of wisdom and transcendence that represents the capacity to overcome obstacles and bring joy and happiness to the family. With bronze umbrella held high, the figure seemed to reign over the display. Lindsay had transformed Mara's bedside table into an altar, and her room into a sacred space. The studio was now ready for the first therapy session with Allan.

When David came for his evening visit, Mara told him about the planned MDMA session. He accepted her decision calmly and didn't express reservations, but to him the possibility of spiritual or physical healing with MDMA seemed like wishful thinking.

When we spoke later, it was clear that he wasn't ready for Mara to face death with equanimity; he wanted her to keep fighting. Nor did he put much stock in my hope that psychedelic therapy would reduce her anxiety and pain. He didn't share my belief that Mara's refusal to talk about death added to her suffering, but he trusted my judgment that the risk of MDMA was low compared to that of her current drugs. Both of us knew full well that there were no other options on the horizon.

The first MDMA session took place on the fourth and last full day of Lindsay's visit. We hadn't known Allan would be available until the previous evening.

"I'm ready to go," Mara announced, in spite of the increase in her methadone the day before. Her dose was now three times what it had been two weeks earlier, high enough to kill a dozen people who hadn't developed tolerance.

Joyce arrived first. She wanted to check on Mara and meet Allan before the session began. Mara's pain was already at four or five on a scale of ten, but her vital signs were okay and she had no palpitations.

Allan showed up a bit late and disheveled in a crumpled shirt and shorts, but fully prepared. He brought capsules of MDMA, music CDs, and a notebook to record times, meds taken, and notes on events as they unfolded. He also brought enough warmth and enthusiasm to put us all at ease. There wasn't a trace of pity in his voice.

"We are going to have an adventure," he said. He told Lindsay it was wonderful that she could be present, and he thanked Joyce for her support. There was an immediate rapport between Allan and Joyce, an understanding that they shared the same sensibilities and goals. It was a pleasure to watch them nod in agreement as they spoke. Before she left, Joyce told me she was confident that her patient was going to have a worthwhile experience.

"I want to be out of the hospital bed," Mara said. "Let's do this in the front room." This was the half of my studio untouched by medical supplies, filled with jade and burgundy pillows in the corners, built-in bookcases, a marble fireplace, and paintings of streams, trees, and skies. Lindsay and I made up an inflatable bed in the center of the room beneath a plaster floral medallion just like the one above Mara's hospital bed—another circle of angels. Allan selected a Paul Horn CD to play and sat on the floor with Lindsay and me. Surrounded by ethereal flute melodies and love, and resting on air, Mara was ready to begin.

At 11:15 AM Mara swallowed a 110 mg pill of MDMA. The therapy proceeded gently. This was an introductory session to explore Mara's reaction to the drug and get comfortable with Allan. We listened to George Winston's piano, and we talked about children and teaching. In the first hour Mara felt a rise in pain (to level six) that her noon dose of methadone didn't help. I could see that she was close to tears. At 1:30 PM Mara took another 110 mg.

Within half an hour she started to notice changes. The first was a huge drop in pain to level one or two. Without prompting, she began to talk about her cancer, her failed chemotherapy, blocks in her body, and healing energy that might break through. She stopped to listen to the music and seemed to flow along with George Winston's slow chording and sudden melodic runs.

By 3:00 her pain was barely noticeable and her pulse had risen from 60 to 80.

"I feel more awake than I have in weeks," she said. When Allan asked her how she felt about her tumors, she told him they were "like kids in school acting out for attention. They need love." She closed her eyes to focus on "sending love to my tumors." She was letting go of the warlike images she had been using fight her cancer.

Is this going to last? I wondered.

At 4:20 Mara told us the effects of the drug were fading. She no longer felt the need for Allan's support and didn't want to keep him from his other responsibilities. "Thank you so much. This was great. I think I'm ready to go deeper next time," she said. Allan hugged everyone goodbye.

The best part of the day was yet to come. Mara wanted to get up and eat. She had a large burrito, more food than she had eaten at one time since before we'd gone to Chicago. She and Lindsay went outside, and for a time they were just two young women talking on a park bench. Lindsay talked about a personal issue of her own while Mara listened attentively and reassured her; it had been a long time since she felt like a friend who could give as well as receive. While she didn't have a transcendent experience and was no closer to accepting her death, an essential part of her identity had been restored.

Chapter Twenty-Two

THE PAIN CAME BACK that night with a vengeance, along with vomiting and nausea and ever-higher doses of methadone. Mara waited until Lindsay went to bed to tell me how she was feeling.

"My heart is fluttering worse than ever. I'm scared," she said. I stayed at her side while the palpitations continued off and on throughout the night.

Lindsay left at dawn. Mara did her best to make it a good departure, just another temporary separation rather than a dramatic farewell. When David arrived to take Lindsay to the airport, we spoke only of the pleasures of the visit and the psychedelic therapy session.

The minute Mara and I were alone, her facade fell away and her symptoms got worse. She was too nauseous to eat, and palpitations fueled her fear. Fear accelerated her heart rate which, in turn, escalated her fear, trapping her in an inescapable cycle of anxiety. I knew her heart rate was dangerously high the moment I touched her vibrating wrist. When my attempts to calm her failed, I called Julie to take us to Brigham & Women's Hospital.

At the ER we were quickly ushered into a curtained cubicle. Nurses checked on Mara and told us a doctor would be with her as soon as possible. We waited two hours in the tiny enclosure. The curtains created an oppressive atmosphere with no insulation from the loud noises of the hospital, the glaring fluorescent light, or the antiseptic air. Somehow, the continuous reminders of emergency care had a calming effect on Mara—so much so that by the time David joined us an hour into our wait, we thought the crisis was over.

When the ER physician finally examined her, he declared that Mara was "awake, alert, and in no obvious distress." Both palpitations and nausea had subsided. Her only complaint was that she was dehydrated from vomiting and lack of fluids. The doctor ordered an IV for hydration, a routine urinalysis, and a CT scan. After the procedures were complete, she was relocated to cubicle 33 in the observation unit, which was quieter but just as claustrophobic as the one in the ER. The coincidence did not escape me: Mara was 33 years old. We were told that if she had no further symptoms she'd be discharged home later in the afternoon.

By late afternoon Mara was ready to leave. She had no palpitations and her heart rate was normal. She swallowed her medications and kept them down. Her pain level was tolerable. It seemed that the hospital episode was over. We assumed that the next person to open the curtain would bring Mara's authorization to leave the ER. All she needed was a doctor to sign her discharge form. She put on her shoes.

The curtains were parted by a slender young resident with caramel skin, an Indian name, and a somber expression. He sat at the end of Mara's bed and faced her.

"Urinalysis indicates a possible urinary tract infection...The CT scan suggests thrombosis...a blood clot...in your left jugular vein," he said haltingly. Then he hesitated.

I'd later discover that he had chosen not to read us the part of the report about the widespread metastatic disease in Mara's lungs, liver, spleen, and nodes.

Eventually he continued, "It looks like you may have a bowel obstruction... And you're in hospice care at home."

The pause that followed was excruciating. This was his opportunity to offer Mara the choice to refuse invasive treatments, avoid prolonged suffering, and go back home. Instead, the young man slumped in silence. He leaned his elbows on his lap and put his head in his hands as if it were too heavy to hold up its own weight. He couldn't look at Mara or find the words to go on. I felt compelled to help.

"Would you like to ask Mara if she wants treatment?" I asked. He gave a slight nod.

Mara spoke up forcefully. "Yes, I want treatment."

The treatment was intense. She was settled into a room on the cancer ward, where she was started on an intravenous antibiotic for her urinary tract infection. A steroid was added after a test revealed an adrenal insufficiency. She was to remain in the hospital, receiving Lovenox injections twice a day to dissolve her jugular vein clot. Mara had been refused Lovenox a month earlier, though it had been shown to prolong life in advanced cancer patients. She wasn't too tired to see the irony.

"I'll do anything for Lovenox," she said, intending the pun on the old song. Her humor was quickly overshadowed by a new round of misery. Abdominal pain, nausea, and vomiting returned soon after her first meal at the hospital. These symptoms added to the evidence of a bowel obstruction and presented a double challenge. Because Mara couldn't hold down anything she swallowed, her pills had to be replaced by IV medications, a difficult task when so many drugs are involved. At the same time, the apparent bowel obstruction had to be addressed.

In the days that followed, Mara was shuttled back and forth between her hospital room and the radiology department. The first scan confirmed that she had a bowel obstruction, and repeated scans were required to monitor the course of treatment. The treatment was brutal. A plastic tube was inserted from her nose to her stomach. She was also given daily enemas, knowing all the while that such "conservative" treatments might not work. She didn't want to think about her other options—either to have surgery or go home to die.

In the midst of it all, Mara was still a young woman who cared about how she looked. "My legs freak me out," she said when she saw how thin her legs had become. Her knees were bony knots that bulged out from her stick-like calves and thighs.

When I asked the attending physician in private about the possibility of intravenous feeding, he said that there were no data to show that it prolonged life in end-stage cancer patients.

"It may feed the cancer more than the patient," he warned. I wondered if the IV nutrition ordered for Mara at the Green Center had accelerated her cancer.

The physical trauma of the hospitalization and treatment seemed to pale in comparison to the emotional distress they wrought. In the hospital environment, Joyce and I couldn't do anything to shield Mara from the dire facts of her condition. When a new doctor asked her if she had been told about her condition, she choked out in a flood of tears, "My prognosis is terminal".

When the oncologist greeted Mara with a perfunctory, "How are you feeling?" she answered that she had felt better.

When she failed to respond to his awkward expression of sympathy, he simply told her, "You have a lot of disease."

"I don't ever want to see him again," Mara said as he left, with more force than I thought possible.

We were visited by two palliative care physicians who were well trained in the art of talking to end-of-life patients. I had spoken to them in private to prepare them for her resistance. They told me there were questions she should hear: Would she want surgery if the intestinal blockage persisted? Did she know that even if the obstruction cleared, the problem was likely to recur? Did she really want to spend her remaining time in the hospital? After asking Mara some amiable questions about her background and interests, they did their best to find out at what point Mara wanted to end treatment.

Dr. Cantor, the male member of the team, began with the best case scenario.

"On one hand," he said, "everything may go well. Your bowel obstruction might clear. You could start eating again and go home."

The woman doctor introduced the second possibility. "But what if things don't go so well?" she asked. "It's important that you state your wishes while you are still able."

"Would you please leave," Mara said. Her chin quivered but her voice left no room for discussion.

Dr. Cantor must have seen the apologetic look in my eyes when he asked to speak to me outside the room. I was stunned by what he had to say.

"I know there is life after death. I'd like to tell Mara a personal story about reincarnation if she would let me," he said.

"I'd like that too," I said.

"If she won't talk to me while she's in the hospital, I'd be glad to come to your home."

"I'll try to tell her. I hope I can. Thank you." I didn't know what else to say. I was touched by his desire to ease Mara's suffering and help her see beyond the life that was slipping away.

At this moment she wasn't ready to talk to anyone about anything resembling end-of-life counseling, and she politely declined the services of both a pastoral counselor and a hospital social worker. Mara didn't want to discuss death. Nor did she feel the need to review her life, forgive herself or others, discover the meaning of her existence, find closure, or say good-bye. Before cancer and pain had consumed her, Mara had loved her life. She had good relationships with her family, her friends, and her students. She felt no need to examine her values or her beliefs, having already discussed such topics with her therapist in California. Yet there was a glaring hole in Mara's therapy thus far—she had not yet been called upon to confront the process of dying itself.

When she went home, Mara didn't want to talk on the telephone. Her relationship with her therapist had ended abruptly when she'd left for Chicago, and Mara hadn't been interested in finding a replacement. She viewed conversations about end-of-life issues as intrusive and patronizing.

On the eighth day of Mara's hospitalization, I went to Brigham & Woman's Hospital—this time as a patient. A few days earlier I had noticed that a bug bite on my hip had become sore and inflamed. The antibiotic my doctor prescribed hadn't helped. I'd been bitten by bugs hundreds of times in the past without succumbing to infection. When I called to report that the inflamed area was now six inches in diameter with discharge oozing from the center, I was told to go to the emergency room. I made a detour to Mara's room to tell her I'd been clobbered by a bug bite and said, "I just needed an excuse to sleep overnight near you."

Once again I was in a cubicle in the ER, but this time I was grateful for the curtains and the wait. The private space provided anonymity and the chance to be alone and release pent-up tears. I didn't care if my sobs were heard; I wanted those who attended me to know that my daughter was upstairs fighting for her life.

The ER staff drew blood samples, took a biopsy of the infected tissue, and hooked me up to an IV that delivered antibiotics. The infection had spread at an alarming rate. I wondered what the chances were that I could die from the infection. It occurred to me that it was no more likely than the probability of dying from colon cancer at 33.

I was contemplating the bittersweet irony of my imminent demise when David stopped by to see me. We exchanged gallows humor, something we hadn't done in the many months of Mara's illness.

"Your live fast, die young philosophy didn't work," I said. "I just might win the race to the end."

"You wouldn't dare." Then, with a droll expression he added, "There are faster ways to go than a bug bite."

I was placed in the same room where Mara had been a week earlier, on the same bed where the young doctor had sat tongue-tied before his dying patient. I spent the night in cubicle 33 worrying about Mara and determined not to abandon her. I thought about the innate desire to die before one's child. Was my infection the result of an unconscious wish to die? Did I long for a morally acceptable way to escape the death of my daughter? Was I getting sick to avoid a failure or an unwanted responsibility? In college and in my twenties, illness had been my habitual way of getting out of uncomfortable situations without sacrificing integrity. As a mind-body teacher, I told my students personal anecdotes to illustrate "secondary gains," the immediate emotional benefits of illness. I confessed that I used to get migraines and severe stomachaches right before obligations I dreaded or exams I wasn't prepared for. I encouraged my students to ask whether secondary gains ever played a role in their sick days.

"When you shed the light of awareness on the dark corners of your psyche," I told them, "you may find better ways to cope with stressful situations." Now I examined my own mental shadows and strengthened my will to live for Mara.

By the next afternoon my infection had responded to treatment. I was switched to oral medication and discharged. Mara had just had an echocardiogram, and I took the elevator up to see her.

I was instantly plunged back into her chaotic world. Mara's bowel obstruction was slowly improving, but her pain medications continued to cause problems. She had palpitations again, and an EKG showed potentially dangerous irregularities in her heart rhythms. After several episodes of irregular rhythms, her methadone was reduced and other drugs were added. Ultimately, a combination of methadone, ketamine, and Oxycodone appeared to be most effective for managing her pain. With the methadone dose tapered to less than half the level she had been taking when she entered the ER, she had no more episodes of palpitations.

Of all the medications Mara received, ketamine was the only one doctors discussed with her. While she had been told about the other drugs she was given, she was asked if she would be willing to take ketamine. The reason had nothing to do with the risk of death—in fact, ketamine made it possible to reduce the methadone and its associated cardiovascular risks. Mara was consulted because ketamine is a psychedelic drug, known on the street as Vitamin K.

"Ketamine is a psychedelic," the doctor warned. "It can cause out-of-body experiences."

"Out of this body?" Mara said. "Bring it on."

We marveled at the caution used to prescribe the psychedelic drug, when the other medications were known to cause disorientation, delusions, and psychosis.

Over the next several days we were encouraged by the improvement in Mara's abdominal condition. After a scan showed no bowel obstruction, the plastic tube was removed and she gradually began to eat soft foods. She was switched back to oral medications to prepare for her discharge. She desperately wanted to leave the hospital.

On her 13th day in the hospital, just when she expected to go home, her vomiting returned. It was caused either by another bowel obstruction or nausea from her pain medications. When an abdominal scan showed no evidence of an obstruction, doctors assumed the nausea had resulted from adjustment to the combination of Oxycodone and ketamine. The nausea soon subsided, but it seemed likely to recur if and when her doses were increased. Mara was asked to consider an intrathecal pump to reduce the level of pain mediations and their side effects. She declined. Mara's memory of the horrific intrathecal trial in Chicago and her fervent wish to get out of the hospital outweighed this particular piece of medical advice.

The following day, two weeks after she had entered the emergency room, and ten pounds lighter, Mara came home. She was tolerating a soft diet and had minimal pain.

She was now on 15 different medications.

Chapter Twenty-Three

WHEN WE GOT HOME from the hospital, Mara needed me to help her climb the four stairs to the front porch. Rather than taking it as a sign of defeat, she made a commitment to rebuild the strength in her legs by adding one squat and one step each day. I was once again occupied with Mara's needs and requests, from food to acupuncture appointments. In the aftermath of the hospital stay, both of us seemed reengaged with life.

Mara now wanted another MDMA session. In two months of hospice care, MDMA therapy was the only thing that had given her a joyful and painless experience and the only thing that seemed to hold any hope for healing. I hesitated, unable to forget the physical crash that followed her first session. I didn't know whether MDMA had precipitated a medical crisis and accelerated her decline or whether it had been unrelated. If it had been related, how could we take that risk again?

Allan and I examined the sequence of events that had followed Mara's first MDMA session. First, we considered whether the drug, which is known to increase heart rate, could have played a role in the cardiac crisis that sent her to the emergency room. Or was methadone the culprit? Mara's symptoms began several hours after the peak of MDMA activity and got much worse after the midnight and early morning doses of methadone. Milder versions of the same symptoms had followed previous increases in her methadone dosage.

There was another factor to consider. MDMA both causes sweating and blunts the awareness of thirst. Since dehydration is known to lead to palpitations, it is this dual property that makes the drug so dangerous among youth subcultures that consume large doses of MDMA (sometimes in combination with alcohol and other drugs) and engage in prolonged dancing at all-night raves. The combination can lead to hyperthermia, extreme dehydration, organ failure, and even death. In Mara's case, methadone was yet another factor in her dehydration.

Some things had changed since the previous MDMA session. After the first psychedelic treatment, MDMA had stimulated her appetite, enabling her to consume more food than she could tolerate given the intestinal blockage. Now, however, the blockage had been removed. She was also on a lower dose of methadone and getting IV hydration every night.

Allan and I concluded that while MDMA probably played a role in the crisis that brought Mara to the emergency room, it was other factors (especially the intestinal blockage) that had led to the lengthy hospitalization. On the other hand, Mara was now much weaker and on twice as many medications. No one knew all the possible interactions between the 15 legal drugs she was on or how they would affect how much time she had left. Allan and I had the same goal as Mara's medical team—to ease her suffering and make her life as comfortable as possible—but we had a tool the medical team didn't.

Allan contacted an expert on drug interactions to help us decide if MDMA would be an unreasonable risk given Mara's changed condition. The physician reviewed Mara's medications and warned us that since Lovenox was an anticoagulant and MDMA increased blood pressure, the combination of the two would increase the chances of hemorrhaging. The doctor suggested that the Lovenox injections be discontinued the evening before the MDMA was administered.

I asked Mara if, all things considered, she still wanted another psychedelic session.

"Let's go for it," she said.

Mara had a lifelong yearning for challenge and exhilaration. As a child, her favorite sports were skiing and horseback riding, activities that frightened me. When she went to college and no longer needed my permission for extracurricular activities, she was drawn to mountain climbing, scuba diving, and whitewater rafting. As a young adult, she led wilderness trips across the country. Part of the appeal of her teaching career was having free summers during which she could test her physical, mental, and emotional strength. She made a passionate case for her point of view in her Master's thesis on outdoor adventure education.

> *Risk is an essential element in adventure programming....Since programs take place in the wilderness where flash floods, lightning, wild animals, and broken bones among other dangers are potential factors, instructors cannot eliminate real risk....To shelter youth from reality, with all its dangers and uncertainties, is to deny them real life. Adventure education programs offer students opportunities to confront life and its unpredictability.*

There was no death wish in Mara's approach to life, nothing reckless in her personal choices, and nothing irresponsible in her leadership.

> *While risk is an essential element in adventure programming, the ideal risk is one that is only perceived to be high, but is actually quite low. The inherent dangers can be minimized through careful planning, well-developed skills, being willing to change course as conditions change, and the ability to let go of a goal that becomes perilous. There's a question that I always ask myself when in a position to decide whether to engage in an activity: If something goes wrong, can I justify my decision to do this?*

As an intelligent and responsible adult, Mara naturally assessed risks and took precautions. She trained me to accept her daring choices and to take pride in her bravery in spite of my protective instincts. She typically omitted the details of dangers she faced until after the fact. She never promised to contact me during her travels and adventures. "If you don't expect me to call, you won't worry," she reasoned.

Cancer had turned our lives upside-down. Mara was no longer able to research opportunities, assess risks, or make decisions on her own. She depended on me. My role had grown beyond working with the medical establishment. Now I was in charge of opportunities outside the law that carried substantial risks—for her, for me, and for Allan. I did all I could to minimize danger. It was no time to be ruled by fear, and I was inspired by

Mara's own courage.

If something went wrong, could I justify my decision?

Mara's second MDMA session took place in early July, a week after she was discharged from the hospital. Although she'd had a difficult night and was exhausted from extra pain medications, she wanted to go ahead with it.

The setting was the same as the first time, with Mara on the inflatable bed and Allan and I sitting on the green rug at her side. At 10:45 AM, she took 130 mg of MDMA. At first she only wanted to close her eyes and rest, but within an hour she was more alert, with less pain, and ready to engage. Once again, the therapy consisted of gentle music and conversation. Allan and MDMA were a powerful combination. The drug fosters openness and intimacy, and Allan had a special talent for breaking through Mara's resistance to medical professionals.

His approach was far from the traditional one in which the therapist doesn't talk too much, insert too much of his personality, reveal his problems, or expose his values. Instead, Allan was Mara's teammate in a life experience, a fellow adventurer as eager to be known as to know her. He was a disarming storyteller of personal experiences that were alternately hilarious and inspiring. Through his stories, he connected to the core of Mara's passions and values. In one story, he told us about a time he visited an animal refuge in New Hampshire.

"The refuge is a haven for dog-wolf offspring that would never make it in the wild but are too dangerous to keep as pets," he said.

"Do they look like wolves?" Mara asked.

"Pretty much. Most of them are husky or shepherd mixes. There was one funny little guy, a beagle-wolf mix who seemed to know he was different, but he knew his place in the hierarchy and got along just fine. Anyway, Fred, who founded the refuge, took me with him on one of his rounds. There were probably a dozen one-acre pens, each with a pack of about seven or eight animals. Twice a day he touches every single wolf, calls them by name, and speaks to them with affection."

"Has he ever been bitten?" Mara asked.

"Nope. He said that every once in while an animal will challenge him, and he has to let it know who's alpha. Fred is a huge, strong guy. He grabs the fur on the back of the wolf's neck, pushes it to the ground, and holds it down until it goes limp."

I wondered if Fred would lose his alpha status or his life one day from an attack. Thoughts of death were never far from my mind. I kept silent as Allan continued.

"I felt really sorry for one sickly animal named Silver who had a huge abscess on his rear-end. Silver had recently joined one of the packs after spending time alone in an introductory pen where he could sniff his future pack mates and observe their behavior. Unfortunately, he hadn't learned appropriate wolf manners: he dug up the alpha female's food. The female attacked him viciously, leaving gashes on his legs and back. The wounds he could lick were healing, but the infected area was out of his tongue's reach, and it looked like he was going to die." Allan gestured with his hands to show the wound was about ten inches in diameter.

"The refuge can't afford veterinary care. I offered to treat Silver's wound and got my first aid kit from my car. I knew it would be painful to pull out the infected tissue and apply iodine. Fred stood by with a dart gun, but Silver seemed to know I just wanted to help. He hunkered down, rolled up in a ball, and let me clean and dress his wound. I camped overnight and went back the next day to change the dressing. Silver came up to me wagging his tail, turned around, and stuck his patched-up butt in my face. Five years later I returned to the refuge and made the rounds with Fred again. When we entered Silver's pen, he cocked his head and looked at me, then bounded forward wagging his tail, jumped up, and licked my face."

Mara's eyes filled up, and she looked at Allan with an expression of love. It seemed the right moment for her to open up to him about her own adventures. I urged her to tell him about her all-night vigil to save Brian, the young man wounded by a water buffalo in Kenya.

She described the walkout from Mt. Kenya, the buffalo attack, and her long hours of banging pots, taking Brian's vital signs, and marking territory with her own urine to survive the night. Her attitude about the aftermath of the ordeal was as revealing as the dangers she overcame. She and the injured student were the only members of the group who weren't angry at the National Outdoor Leadership School for putting them in a dangerous situation. Instead, Mara had defended the program and its leaders. The students had been given the tools they needed to survive. They had been warned that encounters with wild animals were possible, had signed a waiver, had experienced close calls when they were with instructors, and had chosen to proceed. No one had been forced to participate. They handled the situation as well as their instructors would have, had they been present.

"I don't crumble under the weight of intense responsibility," Mara said. "And I can be trusted with another person's life. How else could I ever have known, really known, these things about myself?"

Psychedelic therapy let Mara see herself as much more than a bedridden cancer patient. She remembered who she was. Still, she hoped for an even deeper experience, perhaps a window into her deepest vulnerabilities, and a shift that could heal her.

"I'd like to take more," she said.

At 1:00 Mara took an additional 55 mg of MDMA. Over the next two hours, she talked about private issues—her resistance to intimacy, her fear of losing control, and her dread of betrayal. She described breaking up with her boyfriend and their renewed friendship after she was diagnosed with cancer.

"There's lots locked up in there," she said, putting her hands over her abdomen.

"I don't know when I lost my laugh," she said. "Nobody seemed to notice until last year. A friend told me she loved to watch my whole body shake without making a peep. That's when I realized that I don't even know how to laugh. When I try it feels fake and unfunny. I think it would be a healing thing for me to laugh out loud."

For the first time since she was under hospice care, Mara cracked open a door to her internal dialogue about her disease.

"I don't know if I want to find out about my tumors," she said. "They could be spreading fast or slowly or not at all. There are scans I could find out. I'm open to a miracle, but I don't want to be defined in those terms, as a lost cause. Whatever happens, cancer gave me the opportunity to seek out God, the Spirit."

At 5:00 PM the therapy session came to a close. I was grateful for Mara's respite from pain and encouraged by the deepening of her trust with Allan. She had begun to reveal thoughts she had kept hidden—maybe even from herself—until now.

Chapter
Twenty-Four

THE HOT AND HUMID BOSTON SUMMER arrived quickly. Allan was out of town and there wouldn't be another session for the rest of July, leaving Mara to rely on other resources for managing her pain and improving her quality of life: her family and friends, her alternative practitioners, and hospice care.

Joyce visited frequently to check Mara's vital signs and keep track of her medications, and continued to be our consultant and confidant. She was able to answer our questions and hear the concerns Mara and I couldn't discuss with each other. At one point Mara told Joyce that she didn't want any money spent on her body or a funeral—she wasn't giving up, mind you, just covering the bases. Mara knew Joyce would tell me, but she needed the gentle buffer of her hospice nurse to make her wishes known.

I needed Joyce just as much as Mara did. I wanted to know her assessment of Mara's physical status and what changes to expect over time. I had never helped anyone die before and sought to stave off the shock and hysteria that I knew could follow the unanticipated horrors of death. Predictability gave me the sense of control and confidence I needed to be a steady presence.

In spite of everything, Mara's pain continued to grow. Her ketamine dose was doubled in the two weeks following her discharge from the hospital. The pain interfered with her efforts to build leg muscle strength and increase her mobility; although she had worked her way up to 18 bedside squats a day, she was now afraid to climb the stairs. On one attempt, her pain froze her midway up the stairs, and she had to endure stabs of clenching pain all the way back to her bed where she lay in intense discomfort until her body readjusted to lying down.

Mara's palliative care team suggested that her best option for pain control was the implantation of an intrathecal pump. There would be no trial like the one that had failed in Chicago. This time, it was explained, a far more effective combination of drugs would be administered. Unlike the external pump used in the Chicago trial, an implanted pump would deliver medications directly into the cerebrospinal fluid that surrounded the pain receptors in Mara's spinal cord. The operation of the device and monitoring of the medications would be done by Dr. Roger Ellis, one of the top pain experts in the world.

This time, Mara agreed to the operation. Her stay at Brigham & Women's Hospital was brief. Her pre-operative physical the day before the procedure went smoothly, the implantation took place without complications, and she was discharged the following day in stable condition with ten medications in addition to the three now being dispensed from the pump in her abdomen.

Although the operation was successful and Mara's discomfort briefly improved, there was no dramatic release from pain. During the week after the operation, Mara's pump medications were increased every day, and doubled the following week. By the end of July, the narcotic component of the pump mixture (Dilaudid) had been increased 30-fold.

The procedure that we had hoped would enhance Mara's quality of life ended up only as an additional burden. In order to raise dosage levels, the pump infusion rate had to be adjusted. Every adjustment required us to make a 20-minute trip to the pain clinic. I had to find a neighbor who would be available during the day to get Mara from her bed to the back seat of the car where she would lie down with pillows, keep her distracted during the bumpy ride, find a wheelchair to transport her from the car to the clinic on the third floor, beg the office staff to let Mara go ahead of other patients so she could lie on a bed before her pain became unbearable, help her cope with the wait until Dr. Ellis was available to reprogram her pump, and then repeat the whole ordeal in reverse to get her home.

It now seemed that Mara's only real hope for a better quality of life was psychedelic therapy. She wanted another session as soon as Allan was back in town. Now that her condition was even more severe, and only two months away from the life expectancy she had been given after her initial hospice referral, she asked for a more powerful psychedelic, one more likely to generate a miraculous healing experience.

Allan and I stayed in touch while he was out of town and debated what to do next. We had two options. During my search for a psychedelic therapist, a friend from New York had sent me a sealed package of psilocybin mushrooms with instructions for use. Allan had LSD. Mara believed one of these drugs could provide the catharsis she desired, even though Allan explained that a breakthrough might require a breakdown in her defense mechanisms and along with it a greater fear of death. To minimize the risk, he suggested that Mara take the mushrooms, the milder of the two psychedelics, for the next session.

Psilocybin mushrooms seemed like the perfect choice. They have a long history of inducing mystical states. The Aztecs prayed to the "mushroom god" Teonanacatl and the ancient Hindus proclaimed the transcendent power of the rootless, leafless plant they called "soma." *The Rig Veda* proclaims, "We have drunk soma; we have become immortal; we have gone to the light; we have found the gods."

But we didn't have to rely on anecdotes or ancient history alone—modern science, too, seemed to acknowledge the healing power of psilocybin. On Good Friday in 1962, Dr. Walter Pahnke, a physician and minister, conducted a study at Boston University's March Chapel with divinity students. The "Good Friday experiment" used the gold standard in science: a double-blind, placebo-controlled design. According to a complex set of criteria, eight of the ten who took psilocybin had spiritual experiences like those described by ancient mystics: a sense of interconnectedness with all things, of consciousness permeating all of existence, of unity. It was, the mystics claimed, the experience of unity that allowed individuals to transcend identification with their ego and body. To a person who no longer identifies with that limited sense of self, death is not as threatening as it was before. I wanted that for Mara.

I was not concerned that the Good Friday experiment was limited to spiritually-oriented people in a religious setting. After all, Mara had said that cancer gave her "the opportunity to seek God," and her surroundings had been transformed into a sacred space.

Mara was eager to go forward, and I was willing to be at her side.

On a warm and muggy morning at the beginning of August, Allan arrived for the third therapy session. I opened the sealed package containing the mushrooms and followed the directions. My friend claimed there were enough mushrooms for two sessions. I separated the dried caps and stems into two equal portions, used scissors to cut one portion into small pieces, and boiled them in filtered water to make one cup of mushroom tea. The aroma blended with the fragrance of a cinnamon-scented candle. Mara sipped the brew and chewed the pieces until the cup was empty. We listened to music and waited for something to happen.

There was only one emotional moment that morning. It happened while we listened to an unusual recording, a bluesy jazz piece mixed with sounds of children on a playground. During it, Mara wept silently. I watched Allan write the name of the album and "breakthrough crying" in his notes. He thought the music and the mushrooms had touched a deep emotion. Mara smiled when I told her later. We both knew her tears had little to do with the music or the mushrooms, and that they had instead been triggered by the sound of children laughing on the recording. Mara remembered her students, the teaching she could no longer do, the colleagues she missed, and her lost future. She didn't need a psychedelic to release those tears.

After two hours without unusual physical or emotional changes, Mara wanted to take the rest of the mushrooms. We didn't know if her negligible reaction was due to a loss of potency in the mushrooms, a suppressing effect from her other drugs, or her own emotional resistance.

Allan suggested another option. He had marijuana which, he explained, could sometimes enhance the effects of psilocybin mushrooms when used in the later part of a session. Since it was a safer alternative than a second dose of mushrooms, Mara decided to try it, but she couldn't tolerate the hot smoke from a marijuana cigarette. I became her "water pipe." Between sips of cool water I breathed in the marijuana and quickly blew it into her mouth. She held in the vapor as long as she could. While the effect on me was only mild grogginess, the changes in Mara were substantial. Her pain didn't go away, but her attitude shifted. Rather than describing the intensity of "her" pain, she started talking about it in a whole new way.

"There is still some pain, but I don't feel so up tight about it; it's there, but it's not me." I could see the softening in her face.

"How do you feel about your cancer?" Allan asked.

"There's a snake in my house," she said without any change in her placid expression.

In some traditions, snakes are a symbol of death. So on one hand, Mara's words seemed to convey her awareness of the immanence of her death. Yet a snake can also represent physical healing as represented by the medical caduceus, two serpents entwined on a staff. Or perhaps the snake was merely a symbol for her diseased colon. In any case, it was a perfect metaphor. We wanted to find either a miracle cure or a way to achieve peaceful acceptance. When I later asked her what she had meant, she didn't remember her comment or give it any importance. The window to her unconscious had closed.

Mara was disappointed with the psilocybin session. She had hoped for something more, a catharsis that would heal her. She saw LSD therapy as her last chance for a transformation. She would have to wait until the next time Allan was in Boston.

Three days after the mushroom session, Mara asked me to bring her the telephone. Although she hadn't called anyone since she'd been under hospice care, she wanted to speak to Lindsay. It was her friend's wedding day in California. When the date had been set months earlier, Mara had agreed to read a poem at the ceremony. Lindsay told me they never talked about the wedding again because "Mara couldn't say she wasn't coming."

Lindsay was in the car on her honeymoon when she got the call. Mara's first words to Lindsay were, "I guess I'm not going to make it." She wished the honeymooners well, sent them love, and told them she was happy for them.

Mara's celebratory tone didn't curb Lindsay's anguish. A few days later Lindsay had a powerful dream, the only one she remembered from her honeymoon. She told me it was rare for her to recall any dream with such clarity. She and Mara were on a beautiful beach watching the waves when suddenly snakes appeared out of the sea and began rapidly approaching Mara. Terrified of the snakes, Lindsay cried, "Oh, Mara, I have to stop them." She grabbed a stick and prepared to strike and stomp on them. Mara stopped her.

"No Lindsay," she said. "I want them to come. I'm not afraid of snakes." When Lindsay woke up, she believed in her heart that Mara would find peace before she died.

While Mara awaited her fourth psychedelic therapy session, she made two more trips to the pain clinic. Dr. Ellis decided to change the narcotic in her pump reservoir from Dilaudid to hydromorphone, hoping for better pain control. Four days later, Mara was back for an increase of the new mixture. She was curled up on her left side on the examination table when the doctor approached.

"How are you doing?" he asked.

"I'd feel a lot better if I didn't have to lie down all the time," she said. "I'd be glad just to go upstairs to the bathroom again or to walk across the street to the park."

"I'd like you to make an appointment with Dr. Young, a psychiatrist on our staff. He might be able to help you."

Dr. Ellis didn't address the feasibility of Mara's wish for greater mobility, and I didn't ask any questions. I assumed he referred Mara to a psychiatrist to help her accept her further decline and imminent death. Mara wasn't enthusiastic about the referral, but she asked me to make an appointment for the following week.

"It can't hurt," she said. She thought Dr. Young might know of some new drug that could help.

In the meantime, Mara's strength continued to decline. She ate as much nutritious, high-calorie food as she could without vomiting, though it was never enough to maintain her weight. Since she could no longer increase the number of squats she did by adding one each morning, she began to repeat the exercise twice a day. Because pushing herself up from lying to sitting had become more difficult, she asked me to get her a set of hand weights to build her arm strength. I bought a kit with two-, three-, and five-pound vinyl-coated hand weights and helped her modify the prescribed exercises for her prone position. I didn't believe it was possible for her to get stronger at the same time as she continued to lose weight. It was agonizing to witness her futile efforts, but I couldn't tell her to stop trying.

In the midst of it all, Mara remained true to herself. Her efforts were an affirmation of her character and the legacy she wanted to leave. Her Master's thesis was punctuated with quotes that served as prescriptions for living. Advice from Harriet Beecher Stowe seemed to be fueling her now:

When you get into a tight place and everything goes against you, 'til it seems as though you could not hang on a minute longer, never give up then, for that is just the place and time that the tide will turn.

A quote she included from Eugene O'Neill conveyed the ethic that guided her entire adult life:

The people who succeed and do not push on to [risk] greater failure are the spiritual middle class. Their stopping at success is the proof of their compromising insignificance...Only through the unattainable does man achieve a hope worth living and dying for—and so attain himself.

Mara also wove personal anecdotes into her thesis. She described a turning point when she decided to live her life in a new way. She was 17 and on her first adventure education course. On a day hike up to the highest peak in Utah, Mara found herself unprepared for the physical challenge. She hadn't kept up the recommended pre-course fitness program, and she'd never hiked at high altitudes before.

After hiking several miles and climbing to over 10,000 feet in elevation, I began to feel the effects of altitude sickness. At the top of a pass, from which we would begin our ascent, I decided to stop and let the group go on without me; I stayed on the pass while they climbed the peak. After the group left I experienced a sense of regret and felt that I had given up too easily. This reflected a pattern in my life—I frequently gave up on things when they became difficult. I decided that I would not allow that to happen again. I picked myself up and started toward the peak. I experienced nausea and dizziness and stopped frequently, momentarily giving up and crying in frustration. But somehow I knew that I had to do this for myself, and I continued on. I had nearly reached the top when I saw that my patrol had already begun the descent. I felt crushed, but my kind instructor offered to escort me the rest of the way to the top. With tears streaming down my face I eventually stood looking down on Utah from 13,528 feet up.

On that day I was forced to confront my fear of failure and resultant unwillingness to try my hardest at things. I had always felt that if I didn't give my all to something, that if I then failed, it wasn't a true failure because I hadn't really tried. My potential was always unrealized, and I liked it that way because it left open the possibility that I could be extraordinary. I had never experienced my true limits because I'd never pushed myself. I did not fail on that day, and I did push myself to my limit. I frequently look back on that experience to inspire myself to work harder.

It had been 16 years since Mara made that commitment to herself. If there was any chance that the tide could turn, she wasn't going to miss it. She was giving her all.

Chapter
Twenty-Five

HOWEVER MUCH COURAGE MARA HAD, the waves of illness that washed over her were unrelenting. Diligent exercise didn't make her stronger, an antidepressant didn't make her happier, and Allan was still out of town. Mara began using marijuana more regularly to get some distance from the pain and help her sleep. She joked that I was her "mom bong," but without much hilarity, because she felt bad that the smoke I breathed for her benefit made me groggy. In spite of her previous reservations she started to look forward to her psychiatry appointment. Never one to leave a stone unturned, Mara moved with agility between resources outside and inside the system. She was open to the possibility that a psychiatrist might know a way to reduce her pain.

The day before the appointment we learned that Allan was in Boston and would be able to come the next afternoon for Mara's LSD session. He might not have another opportunity until he returned in September, and Mara didn't want to wait. At the same time, she was interested in a psychiatry-based pain-control strategy. She chose both. She'd go to her medical appointment at the pain clinic at noon and have the LSD session when she got home.

It didn't seem ideal to me. I had hoped to help Mara use the hours before her LSD therapy to prepare. If she could let go of her expectations for the LSD session, if she could be open to the moment without desires or attachment, I believed she would be more likely to experience a spiritual transformation. I wanted to play quiet music and read passages aloud from Jon Kabat-Zinn's *Wherever You Go, There You Are*, a practical guide to the Buddhist practice of mindfulness. I marked passages like this:

Letting go [is] an invitation to cease clinging to anything— whether it be an idea, a thing, an event, a particular time, or view, or desire. It is a conscious decision to release full acceptance into the stream of present moments as they are unfolding. To let go means to give up coercing, resisting, or struggling, in exchange for something more powerful and wholesome which comes out of allowing things to be as they are without getting caught up in your attraction to or rejection of them, in the intrinsic stickiness of wanting, of liking and disliking.

If I had read the passage and taken it to heart before we met the psychiatrist, I might have been more help to Mara. But my own expectations, fears, and resentments accompanied me every time I entered a medical setting.

Joyce and I sat beside Mara in a small examining room in the pain clinic to wait for the psychiatrist. She wanted us with her.

At 12:10, there was a knock at the door. Dr. Young, a slender man with smooth skin and a serious expression, entered and introduced himself. He had a sprinkling of white hairs, making him seem older than his unlined face made him appear. His attitude was serious.

After we completed the introductions, he asked Mara what gave her pleasure and what was hard in her daily life. It seemed like a good start.

"I enjoy listening to music, visits from friends, stories. Sometimes I play games." Her eyes filled up with tears. "But I'm tired of being in bed all the time. I'd like to go upstairs, go for a walk. Every time I stand my pain shoots way up."

"Your intrathecal pump levels are already at the maximum," he said. "You shouldn't expect much improvement. But if we could reduce your anxiety, you might be able to walk a bit further and have slightly more pain control. I'd like you to double the dose of your antidepressant."

Perhaps disappointed that he had nothing more to offer, Mara launched into a discussion of her illegal drug use.

"Marijuana has worked better than the antidepressant," she said. "It helps me relax and sleep."

Dr. Young didn't say anything, so Mara continued.

"The only time I've been pain free in the last two months is when I had therapy with MDMA."

Dr. Young listened with an expression of deep concern. Sensing his judgment, Mara didn't tell him she was about to have an LSD session. Instead, she said, "I'm considering LSD psychotherapy."

"LSD is highly toxic to the nervous system. You could become permanently psychotic," he said.

I was seething. How dare he project his fear and ignorance onto Mara? With all the control I could muster, I pointed out that psychosis was an exceedingly rare effect of irresponsible use.

"Are you familiar with the literature on LSD-assisted psychotherapy?" I asked. "Do you know that before research was banned, hundreds of papers described positive results? That its safety record was far better than Mara's prescription drugs?"

I should have known better than to argue about potential benefits of LSD with Dr. Young. Just two months earlier, an editorial in the British Journal of Psychiatry had pointed out the bias in medical training regarding psychedelics. In the article, Dr. Ben Sessa wrote:

> By 1965 over 2,000 papers had been published describing positive results for over 40,000 patients who took psychedelic drugs with few side-effects and a high level of safety...Despite their history, psychedelics have dropped out of the psychiatric dialogue for today's trainee psychiatrists...In my own training references to compounds like LSD, psilocybin and MDMA were usually followed by statements such as "have no medical use." But I was taught about acute emergencies and the social problems associated with their misuse.

Dr. Young's response to my questions took us all by surprise. He jerked his head repetitively, in imitation of a psychotic patient banging his head against the wall. When he stopped, he leaned closer to Mara and his tone became ominous.

"LSD is far more potent than marijuana or MDMA. It is extremely contraindicated. The fact that you are already taking ketamine makes it even more dangerous."

Knowing that it was pointless to argue, I shut up.

When neither Mara nor I said anything, Dr. Young looked to Joyce for confirmation of his warning. "What do you think?" he asked.

"Mara is a responsible adult capable of making her own decisions," Joyce replied.

Having failed to recruit a medical colleague, Dr. Young frowned and turned his attention back to Mara. She listened quietly as he reiterated his dismal point of view and told her to make a follow-up appointment in a month.

Dr. Young noted his warning regarding the dangers of LSD in his status report. He was apparently satisfied that he had persuaded Mara not to take it. According to his assessment of her mental status:

> *She is alert. She is pleasant. She is cooperative. She has good eye contact. She is intermittently tearful but she does brighten. She is severely emaciated but she lies on the stretcher in no apparent distress. She has fluent speech without any abnormal thought disorder. Mood is down. Affect is slightly depressed with decreased range. She has no suicidality, no homicidality, no hallucinations, delusions, obsessions, or phobias. She is not acutely anxious. Insight, judgment, and abstract ability are fair.*

When we left the clinic, Mara made a few astute remarks.

"Don't worry, Mom, he didn't scare me," she reassured me. "He doesn't know any better. I'll never have to see him again."

My assessment of my daughter's insight, judgment, and cognitive ability was very different than Dr. Young's. She understood that it was futile to challenge the psychiatrist, but beyond that she saw him as a young and somewhat inept doctor who meant well. Her attitude going into the appointment was that it couldn't hurt, and she remained unflustered afterwards. She was ready to move on to LSD therapy. Her calm reaction helped me let go of my anger and eased my anxiety.

I don't suppose there's a psychiatric scale for measuring compassion or wisdom, but if there were, that morning my daughter's would have exceeded mine.

Allan arrived dressed in shorts and a faded plaid shirt, and his arrival lifted the fog that had settled in after Mara and I got home. His appearance contrasted sharply with that of the alarmed and serious gray-suited psychiatrist. We were warmed by Allan's bright smile, calm voice, and enthusiastic demeanor. He laughed at the grim scenario that Dr. Young had described and reassured Mara that her prescription for ketamine was but a small fraction of the recreational dose.

Although Allan knew that a "bad trip" was possible, he weighed the risks and benefits of LSD therapy just as Mara's doctors weighed those of ketamine and her other prescription medications. He didn't discuss the risks with Mara. Doctors don't normally describe the worst-case side effects of medications to end-of-life patients. Mara had been spared knowledge of the potential dangers of her prescription narcotics: hallucinations, respiratory and cardiac failure, and death. Most doctors reserve scary warnings for the drugs they don't prescribe and don't understand—like psychedelics.

Allan discussed the risks with me in private. He was acutely aware of LSD as the most potent psychedelic and the one with the highest potential to elicit fear. However, he believed the potential benefits far outweighed the risks. It was a chance for Mara to have another adventure, an opportunity for a spiritual breakthrough, and a possible means to relieve the anxiety that was intensifying her pain. Moreover, the risk of increasing Mara's anxiety was minimal in our carefully arranged therapeutic setting: The music, ambience, and smorgasbord of medical devices ensured that Mara's experience would be as safe and pleasant as possible.

Allan brought MDMA and marijuana in addition to pure LSD, explaining that MDMA could "soften the LSD experience, smooth out overwhelming visuals, and help maintain a train of thought" and that marijuana could facilitate a deeper LSD experience while using a lower dose of the psychedelic.

Along with the forbidden medicines, Allan brought a stack of CDs for evoking a range of emotions. With a bit of fanfare, he unveiled a marijuana vaporizer, a foot-high machine aptly called a "Volcano." A wide round base tapered to a small cylindrical bowl in which the herb was heated until vapors flowed into a transparent balloon-like bag. Allan explained that the vapor (unlike smoke) is free of undesirable combustion products and cool enough to be inhaled by someone with a fragile respiratory lining. Mara was pleased that I would no longer have to breathe in smoke that made me groggy and contributed to my chronic exhaustion. Although I, too, was grateful, I would miss the tender intimacy of breathing relief into my child.

Allan also brought two books for me. One, Ka-Tzetnik's *Shivitti: A Vision*, describes the LSD sessions of the author, a Holocaust survivor. LSD therapy had helped him recover from the trauma of the concentration camp 30 years after leaving Auschwitz. The other, Laura Huxley's *This Timeless Moment*, is a memoir about her life with Aldous Huxley. It includes a discussion of his prudent, open-minded exploration of psychedelics before they were made illegal, an account of his battle with cancer, and a description of his final hours while on LSD. Unaware of the importance these books would have for me and Mara in the weeks ahead, I added them to the pile of unread materials on psychedelics Allan had brought on previous visits.

This time Mara needed help sitting up, getting out of the hospital bed, walking 20 feet to the blow-up mattress on the floor, and lying down.

At 4:20 PM Mara swallowed 300 micrograms of LSD. We talked while we waited for the drug to take effect.

"I hope I have a chance to bring my daughter Ariel by to meet you," said Allan. "She loves animals as much as you do." He described an evening with dinner guests when the topic of animal experimentation came up in front of his five-year-old.

"She wanted to know what I meant when I said the animals were sacrificed. I told her that sometimes animals had to be killed in order to help people. Ariel whispered some spelling questions to her mom, left the room, and returned to march around the table with a handmade protest sign held high: Animals have feelings too."

We all laughed, but Mara soon turned serious, perhaps thinking that she would never have a child.

"There's so much more I always thought I would experience," she said. She viewed this session as her last remote chance for a transformation, and it was clear that her hope was flagging.

Then Mara asked to listen to music. Allan tried different CDs, from classical music to blues to new age, before Mara was satisfied. She settled into the soothing blend of flute, zither, and harp in "Balanced Music for T'ai Chi." She closed her eyes and smiled. It was good to see her calm and peaceful for a while.

The quiet was interrupted at 6:00 when she took her prescription medications for pain. Mara noted that not much was happening. At 6:30, more than two hours after the session began and well past the time we expected the drug to take effect, she said she wanted a deeper experience.

Allan was amazed that the substantial dose of LSD she had received had done so little. Either the effects of the drug were suppressed by Mara's other medications, or they were held back by her own emotional resistance. Unwilling to risk a higher dose of LSD, Allan offered Mara 150 mg of MDMA. Her response was minimal. She lay quietly and sent love to her pain as she had done in her first session. It helped, but this time the pain didn't go away.

At 8:00 PM Allan put some marijuana in the vaporizer. After a few minutes we watched the bag expand and fill with cloudy vapor. Allan showed us how to detach the bag from the base and fit it with a specially designed plastic mouth piece. Mara inhaled deeply several times until the bag was deflated.

Within minutes, the marijuana opened the gates that had blocked the effects of the psychedelics. She felt tremors throughout her body and her legs shook visibly.

"The pain, it's burning, it's burning," she cried. "But it's amazing how good the rest of my body feels." As the strong sensations gave way to conversation, Mara appeared to feel relief.

We didn't speak directly about death. Instead, Allan told an anecdote about two lifelong friends, older men who affectionately called each other "shithead." When one friend was on his deathbed, the other came to visit. As he entered the room he said, "Hi, shithead." The dying man acknowledged his loyal friend with a smile and said, "No, you're the shithead." He promptly died, thus getting in the last tag and winning their lifelong game. By weaving humor into the conversation, Allan had made death seem less frightening, just one more part of the flow of human experience.

At 9:00 PM Mara decided she wanted to sleep, and our session with Allan ended. He told us he'd be in touch. There had been no glorious cure, no dramatic end to pain, no spark of enlightenment, and no talk of what to do next. Still, Mara had an adventure, a break from the monotony of her restricted life, and an intimate conversation—a gentle opening to talk about death.

I helped Mara prepare for the night. She needed support getting in and out of bed and on and off the commode. I helped brush her teeth and placed her lying down on her back to make medical procedures tolerable. Because she could no longer inject herself, I had to administer the Lovenox. I lifted her shirt to expose her abdomen and tried not to look at the contours of the implanted pump now visible beneath her translucent skin. I searched for a spot unmarked by puncture scars, pinched her belly, inserted the needle into impossibly thin skin, and slowly pressed the plunger. Next I unpacked a bag of saline for overnight hydration and suspended it from an IV pole. The transparent bag was framed by the window where a huge spider plant had once hung. Its spidery offspring used to dangle from the ends of long shoots with no place to take root. Now I connected the long plastic tubing that delivered saline into the port-a-cath in my daughter's chest. I set an alarm for her midnight medications and kissed Mara on the forehead. I replaced the clock on the mantel next to a lovely bouquet of flowers that wouldn't last much longer.

I remembered the first time I was blown away by Mara's precocious intelligence. She was not yet two, and we were in the same room we now occupied, prior to its transformation into my teaching studio. Greenery spilled over mantles, potted plants crowded tables, and hanging plants decorated all nine windows. Little Mara watched impatiently as I moved from plant to plant with a jug, felt the soil, and poured in the right amount of water.

"Play with me," she pleaded again and again.

"As soon as I finish watering," I assured her. When she persisted, I looked down from my stool. Exasperated, I said, "Mara, if I don't water the plants, they will die."

"Good," she quipped. "Then you can play with me."

Chapter Twenty-Six

THE NEXT MORNING, on a mattress next to Mara's bed, I woke to the sound of sobbing.

"I'm afraid to tell you what's wrong," she said. "I don't want you to cry."

"You can tell me anything. I promise I won't cry."

"I feel my will slipping. I don't want to give up, but I don't think I can fight the pain much longer."

My cancer support group had prepared me for this moment. Every Monday night our group sat close and comfortable in a small room on couches and chairs arranged in a square. Husbands and wives revealed feelings they dared not express with their ill spouses or their families, such as the anger that arose when their life partners became controlling or withdrawn. People talked about how to move forward when hope for recovery gave way to acceptance of death. A quiet New England woman overcame her reserve and described the first time her husband of 50 years said he was ready to go:

"What could I say?" she asked. "If I admitted that I was ready to let him go, he'd feel like an unwanted burden, and if I resisted his wish, he'd feel guilty for wanting to leave me. We just cried and held each other. He felt better after that, and I think he was glad to still be here with me."

In the support group, I learned to say the unspeakable. As September approached, I had begun to dread the start of school. Mara didn't want me to take time off or disrupt the work that gave me joy. Although she didn't say it, I suspect she believed teaching would be my salvation after her death. As much as I wanted to honor her wishes, I couldn't imagine being at school while my daughter was dying at home. I didn't want to devote a scintilla of my limited physical, mental, and emotional energy to anyone or anything but Mara.

At a group meeting, the truth came out. "I hope Mara goes before school starts," I admitted. Everyone understood. Nobody judged me. Once I'd let go of the guilt attached to my feeling, it was easier to support Mara. When she told me her will was slipping away, I had the right words ready.

"You're amazing," I told her. "No one could fight harder or be more courageous. How can you not want to go when the pain is so bad? Your feelings may change with the pain. I'll be with you whatever you feel. I'll support you in whatever you want."

I wondered how David would respond if Mara told him she felt like giving up. I worried that he couldn't accept the inevitability of her death and might unwittingly contribute to her suffering. He didn't have day-to-day contact with Joyce or a support group to help him prepare for Mara's final decline. He still seemed to be holding out for a medical miracle, and he continued to seek advice from Mel Reinhart. Mel's last suggestion had been another home trial with Tarceva, the oral targeted therapy she had quickly discontinued because of its excruciating side effects.

David talked with me in private after his evening vigil at Mara's bedside. As we stood together on the front porch, he asked me to give Mara Tarceva again. The request nearly shattered our fragile bond.

"Maybe she'll tolerate it this time," he argued.

"She doesn't want to do any more chemo," I said.

"Just give it to her. Don't tell her," he pleaded. "She just can't die."

Who was he pleading for—Mara or himself? I felt a hot fury, took a deep breath, and summoned the best part of myself to connect with his panic at the thought of losing Mara.

"Do you remember how bad it made her feel?" I asked. It was my turn to plead. "It would only make her suffer more. I just can't do it."

David got in his truck, slammed the door, and drove off. It seemed that our truce was over, and I feared that Mara would see it as a major setback, a personal failure. The one consolation of her illness was the peace it imposed between her parents, a single brilliant victory when everything else was beyond her control.

I promised myself that she would not witness our anger. David could be stubborn, and I didn't expect him to yield in his last-ditch effort to save Mara. If it meant keeping the peace, I was prepared to lie. I would tell him I'd give her the drug.

I needn't have worried. David apologized to me the following day, and we had a long hug. We would support each other in honoring Mara's wishes.

That night Allan came by for a visit with his wife Jill and daughter Ariel, and we were joined by David. It was his first time meeting Allan. Even though Mara reported only positive experiences in psychedelic therapy, he had remained skeptical. Now I sensed appreciation as the two men spoke at her bedside.

Mara was too exhausted to participate, so while David talked with Allan I sat in the studio with Jill and Ariel. I thanked Jill for her unwavering support, for the many hours Allan spent away from his family to help my daughter, and for accepting the risk of legal reprisals. I told her that Allan had told me about a conversation the two of them had soon after he'd made a commitment to work with Mara.

One night Allan had been tossing and turning in bed. When his restlessness awakened Jill, he confessed his apprehension.

"What if something goes wrong?" he asked. "Is it fair to jeopardize our family?"

"Do you feel it's the right thing to do?" she asked.

"Yes," he said, "I believe I can help Mara and her family."

"Then listen to your heart."

Allan was about to leave on a three-week trip, to return after Labor Day. I wondered whether he had brought his family to meet Mara before it was too late. Perhaps he wanted to show Jill and Ariel why he devoted so much time and care to Mara. It occurred to me that the gathering of our two families was his way to say goodbye.

The following day Mara met Dr. Simon Cantor, the palliative care doctor at Brigham and Women's who'd offered to make a home visit. He was the only one I'd told about her psychedelic therapy when she was in the hospital, and he had wanted to describe his own spiritual journey to reassure her that there was life after death. Before she agreed to his visit, Mara made it clear that she wasn't willing to share her innermost thoughts. Her ground rule was, "I just want to listen."

He had the good sense to arrive in casual clothes, leaving behind the urgency and pall of the hospital environment. He appeared to be in his late thirties, with chiseled features, fair hair, a lean body, and a Canadian accent.

Dr. Cantor told us about his spiritual path "from head to heart," beginning with a sweat lodge in Taos, New Mexico. He learned to build *inuksuit* (cairns, or piles of stone) by placing vertical rocks, stacked flat stones, or piles of boulders in natural settings to serve as directional markers and milestones. *Inuksuk* literally means "man of stone that points the way." In the building process, Dr. Cantor learned about balance, control, and letting go. He learned that broken shards provide stability for larger structures. Shards seemed to be a metaphor for the human soul's journey: Broken pieces can be part of a transformation that provides meaning and purpose.

Several months after his experience in Taos, he traveled to Poland for the first time. He accompanied his father, a Holocaust survivor, to Treblinka, the extermination camp where his grandparents had died. After a long walk on the path that had led 800,000 Jews to be murdered, he was stopped in his tracks by a field of cairns standing before him—stone structures dedicated to lost loved ones.

"I realized that I was meeting my own tribe for the first time," he said. "It was a feeling of coming home." After he and his father performed a ritual with stones, they continued to the gas chamber where his grandparents had breathed their last breaths. As he stepped inside, Dr. Cantor felt transported to the end of another lifetime, an instant when he would die if he breathed and die if he held his breath. He felt life-long tension in his throat and neck released. It seemed to him that both his childhood stuttering and the ruptured cervical disk he had as an adult were signs of pain carried over from his past life. He felt that he had been in this place before, as if the tragedy that separated his grandfather and his father had come full circle. He was now present for his father in a way that his father, orphaned as a boy, was never able to experience with his own parents. In this place of devastation, the broken link between generations was healed.

We were moved by Dr. Cantor's story as much as by his willingness to break through professional boundaries to come to Mara as a human being.

After he left, Mara and I talked about what happens after death, a topic we hadn't discussed since her cancer diagnosis. We still didn't speak of goodbyes, but Mara took a breathtaking step forward.

"I still don't know what I think about reincarnation of the soul, but I believe the spirit goes on," she said. "Sometimes I think it may be like scuba diving without the equipment, like swimming free through the oceans. I'm not afraid of death."

Dr. Cantor's story had an unexpected influence on me. Had I not heard it, I doubt I'd have opened *Shivitti: A Vision*, the book Allan had given me about a Holocaust survivor's experience of Auschwitz revisited under LSD psychotherapy. I had been traumatized in early adolescence upon seeing pictures of starving Holocaust victims and learning of the murder of millions of Jews. I had close Jewish friends, an anti-Semitic father, and no way to grieve for the human tragedy. As an adult, images of the Holocaust could trigger nausea and nightmares.

Now, I was inspired by Dr. Cantor's story. If he could find solace in a place where horrors had been inflicted on his ancestors, perhaps I could find the healing I had avoided for so long. The love I felt for Mara as she wasted away to skin and bones allowed me to open my eyes to the deepest form of human suffering.

Laying in bed during the evenings that followed while David was with Mara, I immersed myself in *Shivitti*. I read that when the barracks at Auschwitz were filled to capacity and the crematorium could handle no more, trucks dumped their load of women and children directly into a pit. One SS soldier turned to a Dutch Jew and ordered him to dump kerosene on the pile of living flesh:

> *While the women and children were beginning to catch fire, the SS man walked over behind our row and kicked the Dutchman [who refused his order] in the buttocks. The latter's skeleton-body, like a piece of driftwood, toppled into the flame.*

I quietly grieved for the victims of the Holocaust as I grieved for my daughter. Yet I was profoundly grateful that my daughter, unlike the Holocaust victims, was surrounded by love. As grief threatened to throw me off balance in the days that followed, I repeated a mantra of gratitude: *My daughter is surrounded by love.*

Time marched on, and the relentless cancer wore Mara down. Two more trips to the pain clinic were needed over the next three weeks to refill her intrathecal pump with higher concentrations of medications (Dr. Young's belief that the levels were already at the maximum turned out to be wrong). Mara slept more often than not during the day, experienced recurrent bouts of nausea, ate very little, needed help turning over, and began to have periods of suspended breathing. Intervals of breathing oxygen from a tank were added to her daily regimen. She continued to use marijuana to manage her nausea and hold pain at a distance. It was getting harder to engage and distract her; she just wanted to sleep.

At one point Mara admitted to Joyce that she was losing her resolve. "I'm worried about my parents," she said. "I suck at goodbyes."

By the end of the month, Mara was consistent in her wish to die. "I can't do this any more," she said. "I want to go fast." One evening after she made her plea, I suggested that she might be able to control her time of death.

"You've used your powerful will to survive this long, maybe you can use it to go when you want." I held her hand, the only way I knew to express the love that my anguish might have concealed.

After a thoughtful pause, she gave my hand a squeeze. "That wouldn't be fair to Dad."

"I can call him anytime. He'll be here at your side when you ask."

"What if I couldn't do it?" she asked with a wry expression I hadn't seen in a while. "What if I was like the watched pot that wouldn't boil?"

Chapter
Twenty-Seven

"I never want to go back there again," Mara said.

It was the last day of August, and she was curled up in the back seat of Joyce's car on the way home from the pain clinic. Any movement increased pain, and helplessness drained her spirit. The benefits of filling her pump reservoir with higher concentrations of pain medications no longer seemed worth the agony of getting her to and from the clinic.

At least she was spared knowledge of the pump's postmortem requirements. For this, doctors asked me and Joyce to step into the hall for a private conversation. They told us that that the pump's alarm system must be disengaged after Mara's death. If she died before the next refill date, they would disable the pump before the funeral. In the case of cremation, the pump would have to be removed prior to immolation of the body in order to prevent an explosion. It seemed that the clinic staff didn't expect to see Mara alive again. Numbness was the only reaction I could have and still keep going.

Mara slid faster toward death the following week. Her legs became so weak that she couldn't cross one over the other. She asked Joyce to insert a urinary catheter so that she didn't have to get up. She asked me to listen to the strange gurgling sound of her breathing. I couldn't tell her that the sound was known as the "death rattle," a sign that her throat muscles had lost the strength to clear mucous. Her voice lost its depth and resonance, becoming faint and pure like that of a child. Her breathing was irregular, and her muscles jerked with tics and spasms. She no longer wanted to look at a mirror, and she didn't want to see friends—changes that reflected both her lack of energy and her reluctance to be seen. When she became incontinent, she wouldn't let anyone but me help with hygiene. By directing my actions as if I were an extension of her will, she maintained a sense of control and dignity.

David came over every evening and stayed with Mara until bed time. I was within earshot if she needed me. One night when I was upstairs reading I heard her yell at the pain at a pitch and volume I hadn't thought possible. I suspect the rare burst of anger was her way to avoid collapsing into tears in her dad's presence.

Joyce's daily visits became more crucial than ever. Mara and I continued to discuss issues with Joyce we couldn't talk about with each other. Mara inquired about terminal sedation, the practice of increasing medications until the patient is continuously unconscious. Joyce said she'd help her sleep as much as possible. When Joyce asked what she wanted after she died, Mara said she felt no attachment to remains. She wanted her body cremated, or dealt with in whatever way was the most efficient and least expensive. She wanted her family and friends to celebrate her life rather than have a funeral.

Joyce told me Mara's wishes and listened to my concerns. I dreaded leaving Mara to teach my class, and I admitted to Joyce that I couldn't think about anything beyond caring for my daughter while she was alive. I had made no plans for her body or for a future without her. Joyce reassured me that she would stay with Mara any time I had to be in school, and that whenever Mara died, day or night, someone from the hospice would be there to help.

The one thing Mara addressed directly with me was who should receive her personal belongings.

"Of course you and Dad can have whatever you want," she said. "Give the rest to my friends, and what they don't want, you can give to Aurora." She didn't name specific items for particular people. She didn't want to think about what friends would want, or risk hurt feelings. The only person she named was Allan. "Please do something really big for Allan." I promised I would.

The prospect of continuing psychedelic therapy was Mara's only reason to hold on. She hoped Allan would be back in time for another MDMA session—one more experience without pain, one last chance to love life.

When Allan called to say he was in Boston, I told him Mara was close to death and wanted his help as soon as possible. He agreed to come the next day.

Allan arrived on Thursday, September 8th, just after 2:00 PM. I welcomed him at the front door with a hug. Mara greeted him from her hospital bed, where she would remain. She didn't want to endure the pain of being moved to the front room. She thanked Allan for coming and tearfully admitted, "I know I'm going to die soon."

We discussed dosages, health risks, and potential outcomes. Never before had the decision to go forward been so simple. The greatest "risk" was that her suffering would be over a bit sooner, while the likely benefit was that she'd have some time to enjoy being alive. We decided Mara should start with a 135 mg tablet of MDMA, followed by a second one after an hour.

She swallowed the first tablet at 2:35 PM. After ten minutes of silence with her eyes closed, she asked if it would be possible to wait 30 minutes rather than an hour for the second dose.

"Sure, let's talk about this after thirty minutes," Allan said. "Maybe we can wait just forty-five minutes." Mara rested fitfully as music played in the background.

At 3:40 she opened her eyes and said, "Last time the marijuana started it. Maybe I should smoke some marijuana."

"But you haven't taken the second tablet yet," I reminded her.

"Sign me up."

At 3:45 she took an additional tablet of MDMA. Soon after, her tics and spasms subsided, her labored breathing became easy and regular, she became alert, and her pain vanished. I put a blank tape in the machine on the bedside table and pushed the record button.

"Call Dad," Mara said. I left him a message to come over when he got home from work. It was one of the few times I wished he had a cell phone.

Meanwhile, we joked and told stories. Mara reminisced about the gingerbread houses she'd made with her best friend as a child, and the time she ate a whole one by herself instead of bringing it home to the no-sugar-zone. I laughed about my failed attempts to save her from America's dietary excesses.

"Like when you traded organic fruit and the multigrain sandwiches I made for peanut butter and jelly on white bread with cookies and chocolate milk?"

"Traded?" she said in her child-like voice. "Nobody wanted my lunches. They gave me their leftovers."

"You were corrupted at school, and I thought it was a good idea for you to start a year early." Brookline had a process for evaluating children who were too young to make the standard cut-off date for entering kindergarten, and Mara had been physically, socially, and intellectually precocious. "Do you remember the test you had to take to get into kindergarten?" I asked.

"I remember the story. I wouldn't mind hearing it again."

"The best part was the counting task. The psychologist spread out a handful of pennies on a table and asked you to count them. She said that precocious kids will typically move each coin they count into a separate pile so they don't lose track or make mistakes. She'd never seen another preschool child use the technique you came up with. You swept all of the pennies off the table into your hand, made a money roll in your palm, and counted each penny as you flicked it onto the table." I curled my hand into a fist and repeated the thumb pushes my four-year-old had used to push off coins one at a time. "She said in that single test you not only showed advanced cognitive ability, but demonstrated superior hand-eye coordination and exceptional creativity. You were a shoe-in for kindergarten."

When David arrived just before 5:00, Allan offered us both MDMA. I swallowed a tablet because I trusted Allan's suggestion that it could enhance communication and add to our appreciation of the experience with Mara, but David declined. He said he had meditated before he left home and felt centered and calm just as he was.

I was taken aback. As Mara approached death, I had abandoned meditation, yoga, and regular physical activity—disciplines that had been part of my everyday life for decades. Now I welcomed a drug that removed my exhaustion and helped me be grateful for a few hours. David, on the other hand, had never practiced meditation but had spent the previous hours meditating, praying and chanting *Om*.

Mara became more emotional in David's presence. We settled around her.

"It's so special," she said. "I get to have my mother and father with me…" Her voice trailed off and her eyes filled with tears. It took three attempts before she could get her next words out, each one rising in pitch until she was nearly singing.

"Now that I've decided that I'm going to die soon, I want to indulge in all the things…"

"You can," I said. "You can have anything you want. Most people never get the chance to do whatever they want."

"Chocolate?" she asked. She went from weeping to laughing.

"Should I go out and get you some Fudgesicles?" David asked. "It's a good chance for me to have a cigarette." He was rising to the occasion, letting Mara set the tone with a note of humor.

"Can you get a more gourmet variety?" Mara asked. "Dove bars have superior chocolate."

While David was gone, I went to the kitchen for a moment and left Mara and Allan alone. "I'm their only child," she told him, and started to cry again. I rushed back to see what was wrong.

"I'm worried about Dad."

"Did you hear what he said when he first came over?" I asked.

"No," she said in a high-pitched squeak.

"Before he came over, he was meditating and praying. He hasn't prayed since he was sixteen years old. That was right before he lost his dad. He gave up. Now he's finding something beautiful and pure again, and he knows we're all going to be together. It's wonderful to know you're going to be with us. It makes it so much easier. What you've given us nobody can take away. Your strength and your inspiration has given us strength. It's such a gift to have this good day with you, to laugh together, to love each other."

In the hours that followed we told stories, laughed, sang, and danced. Mara ate the Dove bar with obvious pleasure. The 1964 Temptations song "My Girl" came back to me. I sang with joy and repeated the last two lines over and over throughout the evening: "What can make me feel this way? Talkin' 'bout my girl… My girl."

Mara asked for lively music and directed her dad and me to pick up her limbs and move them to the beat. With her pain gone, she could appreciate touch and movement once again. She told us how good it felt to be stretched. At one point, we each held one of Mara's hands and stretched her arms in a victory pose above her head. Her face radiated with joy at the apex of our family triangle. We were in love with Mara and she with us.

"How beautiful it is to die with my mother and father both with me," she said.

After 10 PM, as the MDMA wore off, Mara's symptoms began to reappear. Allan and I discussed what to do next. We could continue with lower doses of MDMA, keep her lucid, and hope to control her pain. Or we could alternate sedation days with MDMA days to avoid her developing tolerance and maintain the optimum physical, emotional, and spiritual benefits of the drug. As difficult as it was to see her pain return, we decided on the latter, mainly because we were too exhausted to continue. Allan gave me enough MDMA for another session and offered to provide whatever was needed for the rest of Mara's life.

The next morning, teachers at Brookline High met their students for the start of the new school year. I had skipped the preliminary meetings earlier in the week, but had made a commitment to show up for the first day of class. Joyce stayed at Mara's side while I spent an hour at school.

Ordinarily I was excited to welcome my new students. I would introduce the Body/Mind curriculum as a shared adventure, tell some favorite anecdotes from former classes, and take students' photos as they filled out questionnaires about their backgrounds and interests. Over the weekend, I would study the photos, paying particular attention to those faces I might confuse with others and memorizing a special interest for each student. It was important to see the kids as individuals right away. On this Friday, however, I wasn't ready to get to know my students. I greeted them, took attendance, played a video I had made based on previous classes, and raced home to Mara.

I was relieved that she hadn't needed me, having spent the day sleeping fitfully. She awakened only briefly, and she no longer ate or drank. I hoped she would have another ecstatic experience the following day.

On Saturday morning, September 10th, it was nearly impossible to awaken her. Finally, at midday, she was alert enough for me to ask her if she wanted to take MDMA. Mara mustered all of her strength to say yes before returning to her restless sleep—gasping for breath and moaning with convulsive tics and contracting facial muscles. I put a tablet under her tongue.

Her breathing gradually steadied and her body grew peaceful, but she didn't wake up over the next two hours. I called Allan for advice and followed his suggestion that I give her another tablet. Two more hours passed, and I still couldn't awaken her.

David joined us when I told him I didn't think Mara would ever wake up again. We spent the next few hours doing what we did when Mara was awake—telling stories and caressing her, not knowing if she could hear us, feel our presence, or sense anything at all. We ran on autopilot, numb to the avalanche of feelings that threatened to overwhelm us if we paused to reflect on the enormity of the occasion. All the while Mara was still. Her only movement was the slow rise and fall of each breath.

Just before 10 PM I thought of Laura Huxley's This Timeless Moment, the memoir Allan had given me about Aldous Huxley's life and passing. It was as if I'd been waiting for some sign to guide me to a source of wisdom. I ran upstairs to find the book I hadn't had the time or the will to open before that moment.

When I returned to Mara's side I skimmed the pages until a passage caught my attention. I began to read the chapter entitled "O Nobly Born," unaware that the phrase was used to address a dying person in Tibetan Buddhism, a tradition that Laura Huxley explained "gives the greatest importance to the state of consciousness at the time of death." Though I only got to the second page, the last paragraph I read was this:

All too often, unconscious or dying people are treated as if they were "things," as though they were not there. But often they are very much there. Although a dying person has fewer and fewer means of expressing what he feels, he is still open to receiving communication. In this sense the very sick or the dying person is much like a child: he cannot tell us how he feels, but he is absorbing our feeling, our voice, and most of all our touch. In the infant the greatest channel of communication is the skin. Similarly, for the individual plunged in the immense solitude of sickness and death, the touch of a hand can dispel that solitude, even warmly illuminate that unknown universe. To the "nobly born" as to the "nobly dying," skin and voice communication may make an immeasurable difference.

David stroked Mara's hair as I read. Those words, my voice, and her father's caress told Mara that we accepted her passing, that her death could be noble, and that she was not alone.

All at once she began to move. She took her right hand from beneath the covers, reached across to place it in her father's palm, lifted her chin, opened her eyes, and turned her head toward him. She was radiant. In that moment, she was beautiful again. With her last breath she conveyed the rapture of her being, life's final gift to her, and her final gift to us.

Epilogue

IN THE DAYS after Mara died I remembered my vow to honor her spirit. That vow got me out of bed and back in the world, and when I was home alone, it inspired me to write. I began with a letter of gratitude to Laura Huxley.

Many years before Mara got sick, I read *The Doors of Perception*, Aldous Huxley's landmark 1954 book about his experiences with mescaline. The book is a thoughtful study of psychedelics, untainted by the irresponsible hype of the 60s or the irrational war on drugs that followed. It opened my mind to the therapeutic potential of mind-expanding drugs.

Like Mara, Aldous Huxley had terminal cancer and refused to acknowledge the imminence of his death until the very end. His last request was for Laura to inject him with LSD to facilitate his transition. She honored his request and described his final hours in the chapter of *This Timeless Moment* I read to Mara as she passed.

I wrote to Laura Huxley to thank her and tell her about Mara's experience. She published my letter anonymously in the quarterly bulletin of the Multidisciplinary Association for Psychedelic Studies (MAPS). A few months later, I submitted a longer piece which was also published. The essay came to the attention of a *Boston Globe* reporter who used Mara's story as the centerpiece of an article entitled "A Good Death." I wanted people to know why Mara chose psychedelic therapy and the difference it made at the end of her life. Her story offered an opportunity to expose the bias and misinformation that dominates the public discourse on psychedelic drugs. I was ready to begin writing this book.

At first I was determined to document every step of Mara's ordeal, if only to reassure myself that I had done all I could to help my daughter. When I put my memory into words, the agonizing emotions lost some of their immediacy. In the very act of writing I became a witness to the trauma rather than a devastated victim. Along the way, when I felt creative, I wrote about Mara's earlier life and reflected on the meaning of our experiences. Reports of events and footnoted scientific essays gave way to whole chapters on larger themes—love and loss, family, friendship, truth, hope, resilience. In a way that was unforeseen, writing became my source of healing.

2010

*I*T HAS BEEN FIVE YEARS since Mara died. The momentum for psychedelic research is building. Scientists no longer fear the end of their academic careers if they propose psychedelic studies. The FDA and regulators in other countries are now evaluating research proposals based on science rather than politics. After a virtual 40-year ban, scientists are once again exploring the potential benefits of psychedelic-assisted psychotherapy across the globe—in Mexico, Canada, Brazil, Spain, Germany, Switzerland, Israel, Jordan and at several universities in the US including Harvard, UCLA, NYU and Johns Hopkins. The studies concentrate on conditions such as obsessive-compulsive disorder, cluster headaches, opiate addiction and end-of-life anxiety that are difficult to cure or ameliorate with conventional treatments.

The early results are promising. After participating in a South Carolina trial of MDMA-assisted psychotherapy for long-term, treatment-resistant PTSD sufferers, most patients appear to be cured: In follow-up evaluations one to three years after their last MDMA sessions, they no longer fit the criteria for PTSD. At Harbor-UCLA Medical Center a majority of advanced-cancer patients reported improvement in their anxiety and the quality of their lives after psychotherapy with psilocybin. The early results of a similar study at Johns Hopkins are also highly encouraging. There have been no serious side effects in any of these studies or those taking place around the world.

In spite of the positive reports, it will be a long time before the psychedelic drugs now under investigation can become prescription medications. Most of the current research is in Phase II trials (pilot studies with small numbers of subjects) but Phase III trials (multi-center trials with large patient populations) are required before drugs are made available by prescription. Recruiting patients is the most difficult challenge for researchers. Stories of patients who have been helped by psychedelic therapy may be the most powerful tool we have. Mara's experience might provide some idea of what may take place in the future. A patient at the end of her life should be able to have psychedelic therapy at home, integrated with hospice care, and unlimited by treatment protocols that use a single drug and a standard dose. Mara was fortunate to have a caring and knowledgeable underground therapist who used a range of psychedelics at appropriate levels as the circumstances evolved. I am forever grateful to the man who risked his career and his freedom to help my daughter. That gratitude provides the foundation for keeping my promise to honor Mara's spirit.

About the Author

Marilyn Howell, Ed.D., was trained as a biologist and
earned a doctorate in education from Harvard University.
She taught at Brookline High School for three decades,
during which time she created and developed the
first Mind/Body course in public education.

About the Publisher

Founded in 1986, the Multidisciplinary Association for Psychedelic Studies (MAPS) is a membership-based, IRS-approved 501(c)(3) non-profit research and educational organization. Its website is www.maps.org.

MAPS seeks to bring an end to the fear and irrationality that have surrounded psychedelics and marijuana for decades, committing instead to the systematic scientific evaluation of their risks and benefits as treatments for some of the most debilitating and hard-to-treat conditions. Please join MAPS in supporting the expansion of scientific knowledge in the promising area of psychedelic research. Progress is only possible with the support of those who care enough to take individual and collective action.

MAPS' mission is (1) to treat conditions for which conventional medicines provide limited relief—such as posttraumatic stress disorder (PTSD), pain, drug dependence, and anxiety and depression associated with end-of-life issues—by developing psychedelics and marijuana into prescription medicines; (2) to cure many thousands of people by building a network of clinics where treatments can be provided; and (3) to educate the public honestly about the risks and benefits of psychedelics and marijuana.

For decades, the government was the biggest obstacle to research. Now that the government is allowing these studies to take place, the challenge has become one of funding. At the time of this publication, there is no funding available for these studies from governments, pharmaceutical companies, or major foundations. That means that—at least for now—the future of psychedelic and marijuana research rests in the hands of individual supporters.

How MAPS Has Made a Difference

Since 1986, MAPS has distributed over $10 million to worthy research and educational projects. These include:

- Sponsoring the first study in the U.S. to evaluate MDMA's therapeutic applications for subjects with chronic, treatment-resistant posttraumatic stress disorder (PTSD). The results were published in July 2010 in the *Journal of Psychopharmacology*. MAPS is also preparing or conducting MDMA/PTSD pilot studies in Switzerland, Israel, Jordan, and Canada.
- Hosting "Psychedelic Science in the 21st Century," the largest conference on psychedelic science in nearly 40 years. The astonishingly positive attention it received from international news media—including *The New York Times, CNN, USA Today, BBC,* and *Scientific American*—generated an incalculable amount of public support for MAPS' mission, and represents a turn-

ing point in the return of psychedelics to mainstream science and culture.

- Sponsoring a Phase II pilot study of MDMA-assisted psychotherapy for veterans of war with PTSD. At the time of this publication, the study was treating its first subjects in Charleston, SC.

- Sponsoring and obtaining approval for the first LSD-assisted psychotherapy study since 1972. The study explores the effectiveness of this form of therapy for patients suffering from anxiety associated with terminal illness. At the time of this publication, this Switzerland-based study was treating its last subject.

- Designing a study of smoked or vaporized marijuana as a treatment for symptoms of PTSD in U.S. veterans of war. The study will evaluate the safety and efficacy of several different strains of herbal marijuana. At the time of this publication, MAPS is attempting to purchase the appropriate strains from the federal government.

- Waging a successful lawsuit against the U.S. Drug Enforcement Administration in support of Professor Lyle Craker's proposed MAPS-sponsored medical marijuana production facility at the University of Massachusetts-Amherst. The lawsuit argues that by refusing to follow its own Administrative Law Judge's ruling that Craker's license be granted and that the U.S. government should not have a monopoly on the supply of marijuana for research, the DEA is obstructing legitimate research. Despite having received the support of 45 members of Congress, at the time of this publication the lawsuit is caught in a lengthy appeal process.

- Supporting long-term follow-up studies of early research on LSD and psilocybin from the 1950s and 1960s.

- Sponsoring Dr. Evgeny Krupitsky's pioneering research into the use of ketamine-assisted psychotherapy in the treatment of alcoholism and heroin addiction.

- Assisting Dr. Charles Grob to obtain permission for the first human studies in the U.S. with MDMA after it was criminalized in 1985.

- Sponsoring the first study analyzing the purity and potency of street samples of "Ecstasy" and marijuana.

- Funding Dr. Donald Abrams' successful efforts to obtain permission for the first study of the therapeutic use of marijuana in humans in 15 years, and to secure a $1 million grant from the U.S. National Institute on Drug Abuse.

- Obtaining orphan-drug designation from the U.S. Food and Drug Administration for smoked marijuana in the treatment of AIDS wasting syndrome.

- Funding the synthesis of psilocybin for the first FDA-approved clinical trial of psilocybin in 25 years.

- Sponsoring psychedelic harm reduction programs and services at community events, festivals, schools, and churches.

Benefits of MAPS Membership

As a MAPS member contributing $20 or more, you will receive the tri-annual MAPS *Bulletin*. The *Bulletin* contains information about the latest in worldwide psychedelic and medical marijuana research, as well as feature articles, personal accounts, book reviews, and conference reports. MAPS members and supporters are encouraged to join the online mailing list and visit the MAPS website, which includes all articles published by MAPS since 1988.

Donations will be used for funding the highest-priority projects. If you wish, you may specify that you wish your contributions to be used for a specific study. Donations are tax-deductible, and may be made by credit card or personal check (made out to MAPS). Gifts of stock are also welcome, and MAPS offers a number of trust and estate planning options.

MAPS takes your privacy seriously. The MAPS e-mail list is strictly confidential and will not be shared with other organizations, and the MAPS *Bulletin* is mailed discretely in a plain envelope.

For more information or to become a MAPS member, please visit our website at www.maps.org.

MAPS
309 Cedar Street #2323, Santa Cruz CA 95060
Voice: 831-429-MDMA (6362) • fax: 831-429-6370
E-mail: askmaps@maps.org
Web: www.maps.org

Other Books Published by MAPS

Ayahuasca Religions: A Comprehensive Bibliography & Critical Essays
by Beatriz Caiuby Labate, Isabel Santana de Rose, and
Rafael Guimarães dos Santos
Translated by Matthew Meyer
ISBN: 978-0-9798622-1-2 $11.95

The last few decades have seen a broad expansion of the ayahuasca religions, and (especially since the millennium) an explosion of studies into the spiritual uses of ayahuasca. *Ayahuasca Religions* grew out of the need for a catalogue of the large and growing list of titles related to this subject, and offers a map of the global literature. Three researchers located in different cities (Beatriz Caiuby Labate in São Paulo, Rafael Guimarães dos Santos in Barcelona, and Isabel Santana de Rose in Florianópolis, Brazil) worked in a virtual research group for a year to compile a list of bibliographical references on Santo Daime, Barquinha, the União do Vegetal (UDV), and urban ayahuasqueiros. The review includes specialized academic literature as well as esoteric and experiential writings produced by participants of ayahuasca churches.

Drawing it Out
by Sherana Harriet Francis
ISBN: 0-9669919-5-8 $19.95
Artist Sherana Francis' fascinating exploration of her LSD psychotherapy experience contains a series of 61 black-and white illustrations along with accompanying text. The book documents the author's journey through a symbolic death and rebirth, with powerful surrealist self-portraits of her psyche undergoing transformation. Francis' images unearth universal experiences of facing the unconscious as they reflect her personal struggle towards healing. An 8.5-by-11 inch paperback with an introduction by Stan Grof, this makes an excellent coffee table book.

Ketamine: Dreams and Realities
by Karl Jansen, M.D., Ph.D.
ISBN: 0-9660019-7-4 $14.95
London researcher Dr. Karl Jansen has studied ketamine at every level, from photographing the receptors to which ketamine binds in the human brain to observing the similarities between the psychoactive effects of the drug and near-death experiences. He writes about ketamine's potential as an adjunct to psychotherapy, as well as about its addictive nature and methods of treating addiction. Jansen is the world's foremost expert on ketamine, and this is a great resource for anyone who wishes to understand ketamine's effects, risks, and potential.

LSD: My Problem Child
by Albert Hofmann, Ph.D. (4th English edition, paperback)
ISBN: 978-0-9798622-2-9 $15.95
This is the story of LSD told by a concerned yet hopeful father. Organic chemist Albert Hofmann traces LSD's path from a promising psychiatric research medicine to a recreational drug sparking hysteria and prohibition. We follow Hofmann's trek across Mexico to discover sacred plants related to LSD and listen as he corresponds with other notable figures about his remarkable discovery. Underlying it all is Dr. Hofmann's powerful conclusion that mystical experience may be our planet's best hope for survival. Whether induced by LSD, meditation, or arising spontaneously, such experiences help us to comprehend "the wonder, the mystery of the divine in the microcosm of the atom, in the macrocosm of the spiral nebula, in the seeds of plants, in the body and soul of people." More than sixty years after the birth of Albert Hofmann's "problem child," his vision of its true potential is more relevant—and more needed—than ever. The eulogy that Dr. Hofmann wrote himself and was read by his children at his funeral is the forward to the 4th edition.

LSD Psychotherapy
by Stanislav Grof, M.D. (4th Edition, Paperback)
ISBN: 0-9798622-0-5 $19.95
LSD Psychotherapy is a complete study of the use of LSD in clinical therapeutic
practice, written by the world's foremost LSD psychotherapist. The text was
written as a medical manual and as a historical record portraying a broad
therapeutic vision. It is a valuable source of information for anyone wishing to
learn more about LSD. The therapeutic model also extends to other substances:
the MAPS research team used *LSD Psychotherapy* as a key reference for its first
MDMA/PTSD study. Originally published in 1980, this 2008 paperback edition
has a new introduction by Albert Hofmann, Ph.D., a forward by Andrew Weil,
M.D., and color illustrations.

The Secret Chief Revealed
by Myron Stolaroff
ISBN: 0-9669919-6-6 $12.95
The second edition of *The Secret Chief* is a collection of interviews with "Jacob,"
the underground psychedelic therapist who is revealed years after his death as
psychologist Leo Zeff. Before his death in 1988, Zeff provided psychedelic therapy
to over 3,000 people. As "Jacob," he relates the origins of his early interest in
psychedelics, how he chose his clients, and what he did to prepare them. He
discusses the dynamics of the individual and group trip, the characteristics and
appropriate dosages of various drugs, and the range of problems that people
worked through. Stanislav Grof, Ann and Alexander Shulgin, and Albert
Hofmann each contribute writings about the importance of Leo's work. In this
new edition, Leo's family and former clients also write about their experiences
with him. This book is an easy-to-read introduction to the techniques and
potential of psychedelic therapy.

The Ultimate Journey: Consciousness and the Mystery of Death
By Stanislav Grof, M.D. (2nd edition)
ISBN: 978-0-9660019-7-6 $19.95
Stanislav Grof, M.D., author of *LSD Psychotherapy* and originator of Holotropic
Breathwork, offers a wealth of perspectives on how we can enrich and transform
the experience of dying in our culture. This 356-page book features 40 pages of
images (24 in color) and a foreword by Huston Smith. Grof discusses his own
patients' experiences of death and rebirth in psychedelic therapy, investigates
cross-cultural beliefs and paranormal and near-death research, and argues that
contrary to the predominant Western perspective death is not necessarily the
end of consciousness. Grof is a psychiatrist with over forty years of experience
with research into non-ordinary states of consciousness and one of the founders
of transpersonal psychology. He is the founder of the International Transpersonal

Association, and has published over 140 articles in professional journals. The latest edition of *The Ultimate Journey* includes a new foreword by David Jay Brown, M.A., and Peter Gasser, M.D.

Shipping and Handling

Shipping varies by weight of books. Approximate shipping cost per book:
Domestic priority mail (allow 4–7 days): $7.00
Domestic media mail (allow 2–4 weeks): $4.00
First-class international mail (allow 2–3 weeks): varies by country

Bulk orders are welcome. Please contact MAPS for details.
Books can be purchased online by visiting www.maps.org (credit card or Paypal), over the phone by calling 831-429-MDMA (6362), or by visiting your favorite local bookstore.

You may also send orders by mail to:

MAPS
309 Cedar Street #2323
Santa Cruz, CA, 95060
Phone: 831-429-MDMA (6362)
Fax: 831-429-6370
E-mail: orders@maps.org
www.maps.org